W9-COT-332

Religion in America

JUDAISM AT BAY

ESSAYS
TOWARD THE ADJUSTMENT OF
JUDAISM TO MODERNITY

BY

HORACE M. KALLEN

ARNO PRESS

A NEW YORK TIMES COMPANY

New York • 1972

Reprint Edition 1972 by Arno Press Inc.

Reprinted from a copy in
The Library of the Jewish Institute of Religion

RELIGION IN AMERICA - Series II
ISBN for complete set: 0-405-04050-4
See last pages of this volume for titles.

Manufactured in the United States of America

———————◆•◆———————

Library of Congress Cataloging in Publication Data

Kallen, Horace Meyer, 1882-
    Judaism at bay.

    (Religion in America, series II)
    1. Judaism--Addresses, essays, lectures. I. Title.
BM45.K35 1972   296   74-38451
ISBN 0-405-04071-7

JUDAISM AT BAY

JUDAISM AT BAY

ESSAYS
TOWARD THE ADJUSTMENT OF
JUDAISM TO MODERNITY

BY

HORACE M. KALLEN

1932
BLOCH PUBLISHING CO.
"The Jewish Book Concern"
NEW YORK

PRINTED IN THE UNITED STATES OF AMERICA
BY THE VAIL-BALLOU PRESS, INC., BINGHAMTON, N. Y.

CONTENTS

v

I

FOREWORD: JUDAISM IS AT BAY

Judaism is at bay.

There is a sense in which all religions are at bay in the world where science and industry have crowded them from the center to the periphery of human interest. And in relation to those major powers of modernity, Judaism participates with the other religions in the emotional disturbance they sustain. It also is distraught under the secularizing pressure of the modern world. But Judaism, besides being one of the religions of western civilization, is the religion especially condemned and outlawed within that civilization ever since Christianism became the official faith of the polities of Europe. In the days when there was no science, and skilled industry was mystery, magic and deviltry, Judaism was walled into the ghetto by Christian law, with no door out except destruction. So the walls were security as well as imprisonment. Within the ghetto Judaism retained the primal organic relationship to the fullness of national life which is characteristic of religion in antiquity. For this reason it passed through the Middle Ages and into the unprecedented conditions of the modern world with the essential traits of the pre-Christian pagan religions of civilized Europe. Judaism entered modernity considerably monasticized, but still positive, national, this-worldly, concerned about the good life here at least as much as about the saved life beyond.

Certain disadvantages accompanied these advantages.

1

If Judaism retained its organicity, it did so at the expense of its relevancy. When the spirit of modernity broke the walls of the ghetto and the religion of the Jews was confronted with the secular gains of the centuries, it was found to be largely a survival, unequipped, indeed, unfit, to cope with the problems of adjustment in an environment where science, humanism, democracy and industry were the prevailing social aspirations and the increasingly prepotent social powers.

The process of adjustment to the new world, which began late in the eighteenth century, led to division in the internal economy of the life of the Jewish people. Antique pagan organicity gave way to conflict and fission. Secularization set in. Religion was segregated from the other institutions and interests of community life. The process of internal division and readjustment came to be known as Haskalah. Haskalah may be translated Enlightenment. It amounts to the fact that the fused religious and secular components of Jewish life separated out and moved away from each other; that the secular acquired not only independence, but preeminence based on superior power: that it turned on religion for its deficiencies and belittled or ignored its virtues. Thus Judaism was crowded into a corner, not only by the anti-Jewish religion of non-Jews, but by the secularizing ardor of Jews entering upon a belated Jewish Renaissance. Judaism was more than ever at bay.

To survive, it endeavored in one direction to increase its mobility and thus recover its superiority. This endeavor is what the reform movement in Judaism sums itself up to. It consists essentially in a lightening of the "yoke of the law" to the point where its bearers do not know they are supposed to be bearing it. To be a Judaist of the reformed sect places on the believer about as little responsibility in worship, ceremonial, and conduct as a cult well can. . . . In the other direction Judaism endeavored to harden its practices into a protective integument like a turtle's shell. It contracted into the rigid ritualism of the Agudath Israel.

Both the mobile and the contracted modes of defense cut themselves away from the secular center of Jewish life. Both nevertheless appear to be impotent against the insaturable solvents of modernity. Regardless of the fact that anybody who counts himself as a Jew is classed by the census-taker as a Judaist, the synagogue is becoming an empty shell. Judaism is left more and more to the interest and care of professionals trained—I almost wrote mis-trained, and perhaps I should write mis-trained—for the purpose. Jews in common with the other children of industrial society are secular-minded, skeptical, and this-worldly; with faith in the discovery and control of nature rather than the contemplation and management of God. Only at times when resurgent anti-Semitism alarms them do they think again of the religion of the Jews.

For this reason the number of sects in modern Judaism has been increasing at a greater rate than in the whole millennium before. No sooner was reform established than it encountered secession and was faced with the organization of conservative Judaism. Conservatism was within a generation confronted by the attitude and the program which find their high place in the religious philosophy of Mr. M. M. Kaplan. That was soon followed by a point of view whose spokesmen are Stephen S. Wise and his organization, while on the outskirts there play the Judaistic echoes of Christian Science called "Jewish Science." The frame of reference for all of these sectarian developments within Judaism seems to be Jewish nationalism. They define themselves for Jewish life by their attitude toward it. and the transformation of attitudes tells the story. Isaac

M. Wise called Zionism an "idiosyncrasy of late immigrants from Europe." His successors, at their last convention, added Hatikvah into their hymnal, and speak with
authority in the councils of Zionists. Many of the temples
are even beginning to have more Jews than Christians in
their choirs, and all of them evince a marked tendency to
restore excised ceremonial in one form or another. Many
young men preparing for the rabbinate, and young rabbis
still unhurt by the predicament of their position, give signs
of great doubt concerning the vocation of "spiritual
leader." The feeling is strong among the more sensitive
members of the profession that all is not as it should be
with the state of Judaism.

And the feeling is justified. For Judaism has been alienated from the Jewish people. Its upkeep is today the concern of a class above a certain income level rather than of
the masses, and by and large this class is concerned only
to the point of supplying the cost of the plant and of the
"spiritual leader" through whose professional expertness
they may discharge their religious obligations. As I observed long ago, they practise their Judaism by proxy. . . .

The essays here brought together signalize episodes in
the struggle of Judaism at bay. Many have been printed
before. Others have been written to round out the argument of this book. Certain readers will regard all as blows
in attack; to the more understanding they will, I trust,
appeal as efforts in defense. That is what they are to me.
For I am certain that if Judaism is to survive, it can
survive only in its older form as organic to the life of the
Jewish community. *Gabbaim* and *rabbonnim* to the contrary notwithstanding, the Jewish way of life is no longer
a religious way of life. Judaism is no longer identical with
Jewishness and Jewishness is no longer identical with
Judaism. Jewishness—I prefer to say, Hebraism—is a

focus of modernity. It is the Jewish way of life become necessarily secular, humanist, scientific, conditioned on the industrial economy, without having ceased to be livingly Jewish. Judaism will have to be reintegrated with this secular, cultural form of community which is Jewishness if Judaism is to survive. Such a reintegration requires the dissolution of the intransigency both of the reformers and the Agudath Israel. As the record since the War shows, events are of themselves attending to this matter. But a little realistic thinking, a little attention to conditions as they are, to the dynamic factors in the situation, could clear the air, dispel illusion, save much heartbreak, much waste, and much unhappiness. This is my reason for responding at last to the requests which have come to me in numbers through the years from many Jews, clerical as well as lay, concerned about the survival of Judaism, that I assemble and republish my endeavors in the field. That they can effect more than the trembling of a leaf, I am not so vain or so deluded as to hope. Yet even against the weight of experience, hope insists on springing still. . . .

I am indebted for permission to reprint, first to the late Joseph Jacobs, editor of the *American Hebrew,* on whose urging many of these essays were written; then to the editors of *The Menorah Journal, The New Republic, The Nation, The Survey, The Jewish Center,* and *Opinion.* I have tried to keep as nearly as possible to the original tone and form. Where the material seemed dated by lapsed conditions I have made changes. But the changes are very few. There is also a certain iteration for which I make no apology. Events themselves reiterate, and crises repeat themselves, *crescendo.* Not a single issue here taken up has been brought to any termination, even the termination of death. They are all, if anything, more ominously alive than they were twenty years ago.

To my sister, Miss Frances Kallen, I am greatly indebted for help with the text and the proof; I hardly
know how, amid the great pressure of my regular tasks, I
should have gotten through without her. Similar acknowl-
edgments are due to my friend and former pupil, Professor Harry A. Wolfson.

March, 1932

II

HEBRAISM AND CURRENT TENDENCIES
IN PHILOSOPHY

Since the publication of Mr. Matthew Arnold's Culture and Anarchy, the contrast between Hebraism and Hellenism has been a commonplace of the critic and a fruitful source of platitude for the learned pulpit of "reform" Judaism. "The aim and the end of both Hebraism and Hellenism is . . . one and the same . . . that we might be partakers of the divine nature. . . . Still they pursue this aim by very different courses. The uppermost idea with Hellenism is to see things as they really are; the uppermost idea with Hebraism is conduct and obedience. Nothing can do away with this ineffaceable difference." *

This 'ineffaceable difference" has been made much of, now to the derogation of Hellenism, now of Hebraism. It is the apparent overemphasis of Hebraism that calls forth Mr. Arnold's essay. It is the underemphasis of Hellenism that gives birth to much of the satire of Heine. Neither of them, says Arnold, is "the *law* of human development as their admirers are prone to make them; they are each of them *contributions* to human development. . . . The nations of our modern world, children of that immense and salutary movement which broke up the pagan world, inevitably stand to Hellenism in a relation which dwarfs it, and to Hebraism in a relation which magnifies it."

Now, whatever one may think of the relative weight of

* Culture and Anarchy. Chapter IV.

these "contributions to human development," the description of them which Mr. Matthew Arnold supplies, is like all his proper contributions, true only in the schoolmaster's sense of true. It represents a conventional, traditional attitude, and the effect of tradition is invariably to harden living fact into dead literature and so to falsify its essence.

In truth, Hellenism is not concerned with "seeing things as they really are," but with seeing things as they *ought to be;* Hebraism is not concerned with conduct and obedience, it is concerned with making the best of a bad job. The aim of Hellenism is *perfection;* the aim of Hebraism is *righteousness.* Mr. Arnold identifies the two; but they are not and never can be identical. To be saved from a menacing environment is one thing; to exercise your power to the utmost is quite another. The most representative Hellenic book is Plato's Republic; the most representative Hebraic book (opinion to the contrary notwithstanding) is Job. The great Hellenic virtues which constitute the theme of the Republic are temperance and justice. The great Hebraic virtues, those which are the lesson of Job, are faith, hope and charity. Temperance and justice mean the perfect use of what is already possessed; they mean order, balance, symmetry. Faith, hope and charity mean dearth, strain for the unpossessed, something off its balance and struggling to regain it. The contrast is the contrast between "nothing too much," and "I know that he will slay me; nevertheless will I maintain my ways before him." The latter represents the invincible loyalty of life to itself, in the face of overwhelming odds. The former is bothered by no protean environment ominous with evil; it needs only the ordering of goodness.

Such fundamental moral differences imply a still profounder difference,—a difference in metaphysical insight. The contrasting virtues are instruments or modes of adaptation to contrasting environments. Historically, these may be defined in terms of climate, political relationships, internal and external cataclysms. But we do not seek the cause of vision, we seek its essence. And that essence was for the Greek, structure, harmony, order immutable, eternal; for the Hebrew, flux, mutation, imminence, disorder. The Greeks saw their world as a composition—a hierarchy of ideas, or forms, each having an especial place in the whole; to them no thing could be explained save by the larger unity to which it belonged. The Jews saw their world as a flux, in which events occurred freely according to no predetermined plan. Sin got its punishment, virtue its rewards. But no man was immutably sinful, no divine fiat eternal and unalterable. There is room for atonement, for a readjustment and a new life; there is a chance "to be born again." For the Greeks, what was from the beginning shall be to the end. The thing is exemplified best in the greater tragedies, which portray the inexorable working of ancestral curse. Destiny is necessary. For the Hebrews, an alteration of life means an *alteration of destiny*. A "repentant" man means a "forgiving" God. In a word, for the Greeks, change is unreal and evil; for the Hebrews the essence of reality is change. The Greek view of reality is static and structural; the Hebrew view is dynamic and functional.

Let, however, no sermonizer see in this fact cause for pulpit congratulation. The Hebraic vision of reality was, I believe, the truer of the two, but it was not the more civilized. The metaphysic which is implied and even expressed in the conceptions of that very primitive people, the Arunta, is Hebraic. The metaphysic of all barbarous people is Hebraic. To achieve the conception of an eternal order and a static universe, in the face of the very obvious flux of the daily life, is a feat magnificent indeed. The

Hebrews were not right because they had attained intellectual efficacy. They were right because they had *not* attained to intellectual efficacy. They were right because their vision was frankly innocent and unsophisticated. When they began to think metaphysics at all, they immediately began to Hellenize. The history of their philosophy, as that of the whole Christian world, is the history of an attempt to subordinate the prophets to Plato, revelation to Aristotle. From Philo to Mendelssohn, as from St. Augustine to Hegel, the attempt has been to make the dynamic and functional character of the universe an aspect, a mere appearance of the static and structural, to explain the part by the whole, mutation by identity. Philo sees in the precepts of the prophets the eternal ideas of Plato. Hegel sees in the separate aspects of the "dialectic process" a mere appearance of a processless and immutable absolute. In philosophy at least, the nations of our modern world have stood to Hebraism in a relation which dwarfs it and to Hellenism in a relation which magnifies it. It is easily demonstrable that the relation holds not only in philosophy, but in innumerable other intents of life—that all which Hebraism supplied that was potent, in the history of nordic Christian civilization, was merely a new language for an unabandoned vision, that the gigantic reconciliation which Christian institution and thought attempted between Hellenism and Hebraism never took place, that Hebraism has never dominated European life to the degree in which Hellenism has dominated it, that the "supremacy" of Hebraism is, if one reads the signs of the times aright, yet to come. But this larger thesis must be passed by; our present purpose is to note that philosophy and science at least were until the middle of the nineteenth century, predominantly Hellenic. To be Hellenic in philosophy is to deny that change is ultimately real, to define any part by the "whole" to which it belongs, to see the universe as static.

In science, to be Hellenic is to understand the subject of research as eternal and immutable substance, as forms, genera, species, varieties, existing eternally in their Aristotelian classifications. Thus for biology, parent and offspring, of necessity and according to law, conformed to the same type and were measurable by an immutable standard. The death-blow to scientific Hellenism was given by Darwin. The very title of the book which challenges the principle of the permanence of species, indicates its utterly revolutionary character. "The Origin of Species!" —to give species an origin is to abandon the notion of the eternity of forms and of the structural order of the universe. It is to espouse the flux, to allow for the reality of individuals as against classes, to allow for genuine freedom and chance in the world, to insist on the concrete instance rather than on the general law—in a word, to give an overwhelming scientific background to the Hebraic as against the Hellenic visions of the nature of reality. The crux of Darwinism lies in the two principles of "spontaneous generation" and the "survival of the fit." These two principles have not altered; nor amid all the *pros* and *cons* Darwin's theory gave rise to, have they been really shaken. The latest fashion in evolutionary biology—De Vries' doctrine of "mutations,"—does not challenge them, it only asserts them less modestly than they assert themselves.

Official philosophy took little note of the tremendous philosophical implications of Darwinism. Nietzsche, indeed, with vehement unintelligence, tried to apply it to morals and various materialistic "evolutionary" monisms sprang up as if "evolution" and "monism" were not contradictory terms. The great task of developing the philosophy of evolution in the Darwinian sense of the word—and that is a very different sense from the popular and philosophic one—is the affair ⌐f William James, an American, and Henri Bergson, a Jew of France. "The teaching of these two men—a teaching of which James is the inspirer and originator and to which Bergson gives the amplest and most adequate expression—rehabilitates the Hebraic vision of reality utterly."

Pragmatism, as the "new" philosophy of James is called, is a "new name for old ways of thinking." Its radical contribution to thought is the introduction of the postulates of "spontaneous variation" and the "survival of the fit" into the inner nature of the universe, in metaphysics, and into the world of ideas, in the theory of knowledge. Of all things, it must be said "by their works shall ye know them!" A thing is what it does. An idea is true if it leads prosperously, if it has a genuine survival-value, if it endures, by working, in the flux—if it is fit. Morally, the attitude of man must be "melioristic." The world is all conflict; it contains evil, it is full of menace and danger. But these are not eternal. Man is genuinely free, he can change his world and himself for the better. He can ameliorate it by his very faith. In a universe rich with actual contingencies, faith and works even of so small an item as man, may be and often are, pregnant with tremendous human and even cosmic consequences. You are, therefore, entitled to believe at your own risk, and since the world is in flux, the mere existence of that belief may be just the one needed factor to make its object real. Nothing is eternally damned, nothing eternally saved; the contributing value to the validity of your beliefs, to the strength of your life, is as much yourself as the environment to which you must adapt yourself. But this is only the modern way of asserting in an unfortuitous environment "I know that he will slay me, nevertheless will I maintain my ways before him." The very act of maintaining one's ways may render the slaying impossible. To believe in life in the face of death, to believe in goodness in the face of evil, to hope for better times to come, to work at bringing them about—that is Hebraism. Whether Biblical or Talmudic, that is the inner history of Jews, from the beginning to the present day—an optimistic struggle against overwhelming odds. That is Hebraism, but it is the Hebraism, not of childhood and innocence; it is the Hebraism of old age and experience. It is a vision of the world that has been tested in the furnace and come out clean. Judaists cannot be accused of it. In their practical philosophy and theology they became Hellenists a thousand years before Claude Montefiore. What current rabbinism calls Jewish philosophy, is not Jewish philosophy at all. It is a transformation of the Jewish insight by alien forms, just as the rest of modern Jewish life is a transformation of spiritual integrity by financial materialism.

Yet, strangely enough, the most adequate exponent of this tested and purified philosophic Hebraism, is himself a member of the Jewish people. Henri Bergson was born in Paris in 1859. "His career"—I quote from lecture 6 in James's "A Pluralistic Universe,"—"has been the perfectly routine one of a successful French professor. Entering the *école normale superieure* at the age of twenty-two, he spent the next seventeen years teaching at Lycées, provincial or Parisian, until his fortieth year, when he was made professor at the said *école normale*. Since 1900 he has been professor at the College de France, and a member of the Institute since 1906."

"His vision is stated in three books: Essai sur les donnees immediates de la Conscience (1889), Matiere et

Memoire (1896), l'Evolution Creatrice (1907), each written superbly, enticingly. His style seduces you, and bribes you in advance, to become his disciple. It is a miracle, and he is a real magician."

I cannot here go into the philosophic development of Bergson's vision. It is subtle, exceedingly, it is extraordinarily original. He differs from Prof. James both in emphasis and in substance. James stresses the epistemological and ethical aspects of philosophy; Bergson, the metaphysical. Like James, he finds knowledge, ideas, concepts to be entirely practical. Their existence is justified by their use. But because they are practical, they stand *between* the mind and the actual reality and to some degree they falsify the latter. They are *not* identical with the actual reality for which they stand and of which they are an aspect. The reality is a *moving act*. Ideas are cinematographic portraits of it. Its thickness, its richness and above all, its *motion,* are not represented in the pictures. In the pictures you have merely a string of positions through which the motion, the life of reality, has passed. These are static and dead. They are mere instances, mere appearances of the propulsive flux of the universe, of its *élan vital.* You are face to face with reality, not when you are reasoning about it, not when you have *ideas* of it, but when you are *living* through it. The inner aspect of things is found in the process, the *immediate* shock and recoil of the daily life. There, in *doing* you get at the *élan vital* of things and really know and possess them as they are.

Now, this is exactly the opposite of the Hellenic view. The Hellenic insight finds reality alone in the static idea, in the eternal, the immutable structure of things. For Bergson this structure is only an incident, a mere instant or position through which the *life* of the world passes. Change and not immutability is found real; the static and not the dynamic is found to be "mere appearance," unreal. But such a finding is the essential finding of Hebraism. In philosophic thought, it is exceedingly recent, but promises to be philosophically dominant. The Jamesian and Bergsonian versions of the metaphysic of the flux, the metaphysic of Hebraism, open a new era in the history of philosophy—an era in which the old order—Hebraism subordinated to Hellenism—is reversed; an era which will understand the structure of the world as a passing instance in its dynamic flow; its form as an ephemeral expression of its own *élan vital*.

1909

III

ON THE IMPORT OF "UNIVERSAL JUDAISM"

I had not very long ago the interesting experience of hearing, at the Menorah Society, the discourse of a clerical gentleman, whose very impressive person and manner are intensely vivid to me whenever I hear the word "universal" mentioned in connection with the word "Judaism." I do not recall whether "universal Judaism" was the title of his paper, but I remember clearly that the phrase was used an infinite deal—though I have only the vaguest and most confused notion as to its purport or significance. What impressed me deeply was the fact that I was here face to face with a person who was in serious earnest defending a thing called "universal Judaism," whatever that may be, in connection with another equally indeterminate thing called "the mission of Israel." I had, of course, seen both phrases before, in essays in magazines and newspapers, and I had heard them before from rabbis. But I had paid them only cursory attention, as in the first place neither writers nor speakers seemed to me really serious about them; and in the second place, both phrases seemed so obviously self-contradictory and unhistorical. The love of the unthinking for these phrases, I could see, clearly enough, was due to the fact that they were unthinking; the love of their professional advocates I assigned to less noble causes—not without reason, I am justified in believing. But here was a man who obviously had thought, how-

16

ever illogically, and whose use of the expressions "universal Judaism" and "mission of Israel" betrayed genuine and deep emotion. Both his attitude and his logic intrigued me. I cast about for explanation. As I happen personally to have no liking for orthodoxy as against reform, or the *tertium quid* called "conservative Judaism," as against either, I may honestly assume that my explanation was made without bias, and I venture to present its results in the hope of adding a little to the gaiety occasioned by the recent deliberations of the reformed rabbis in New York.

I shall first speak of the logical meaning of the term "universal" and the effect of its application to "Judaism." Then I shall say something about the psychological basis of this application.

I

It is interesting to note, first of all, that "universal" is fundamentally a Greek and not a Jewish notion. Indeed I may safely go so far as to assert that ancient Hebrew contains no equivalent for it and that the equivalents to be found in rabbinic literature are of non-Hebraic derivation—either Hellenistic or Arabic. But I am not a philologist and do not pretend to say with certainty anything more than that the notion "universal" is distinctly un-Hebraic. That, of course, offers no valid objection to its present function and status in Judaism, but it does offer a presumption against its justification by history. And this presumption seems to me logically validated by the story of Judaism as a cult.

If you ask the man on the street for the meaning of "universal," the chances are that he will stare at you for a minute and then will stutter, "Why, er—er—common, general—" And that will be a good answer, But like all good answers, insufficient. The commonest intention of "universal" is indeed commonness or generality. But commonness and generality are altogether matters of degree and an opinion or a religion may be common to two men or two million. The universalists among Jews would, I suspect, be altogether unwilling to base the universality of their Judaism on the number of its adherents. Such a universality would not be worth having, for it would not be different from the universality of any belief or opinion: "rabbis are reasonable," or "two and two equal four." The last proposition has very enviable universality, for everybody who can count believes it; but nobody will be willing to say that it is "univeral" because everybody believes it. They will say rather that everybody believes it because it is universal. In either case, Judaism has not that kind of universality, for many people do not believe in Judaism, hence excluding it from universality by privation; and again Judaism is not "universal" in nature or character, since not everybody believes in it.

There is a second meaning of "universal" which may be nearer to the thing the rabbis have in mind, though I am not aware that it has ever been made explicit. The first meaning has, I suspect, been one of the things they commonly thought of, i.e., capacity for being believed by all men. The second intention of "universal" is what the logicians call "necessary" or "valid." In this sense of the word, natural law, i.e., the laws of motion, gravitation, the second law of thermo-dynamics, are "universal." But all that necessity or validity here means, is the identity of a thing or an action with itself, in any place or at any time. So, for example, the "law" of gravitation means that falling is falling, whether it occurs in Australia, in Newark, or at the North Pole. Space is universal in this sense; so is time, red, theft, love, anything you can think of. Judaism, in this intention of "universal" is not more so than Christianity, Shinto, or the totemism of the Arunta. It is one of the infinity of such universals which make up our world. It is a kind of universality no more precious and distinct than the other.

Then there is the conception of the "universal" as the typical, the ideal in the Platonic sense of the word. In this meaning, "universal" is used in opposition to the concrete and particular. So, for example, the idea or definition of Man is opposed to particular men. Particular and individual men are so because they are at least numerically diverse, because they exist in particular places and at separate times, because they live and die, because they change, they have a history. The type, Man, doesn't exist anywhere in particular, or at any time whatsoever; it has no history and no life. It is one and immutable. Now, I dare say, there might be found in some insuperable Platonic otherworld a type, Judaism, which has the same nature as the type, Man. But I have until latterly, been very reluctant to believe that anybody existed who was silly enough to assert that any particular form of Judaism existing in *this* world was identical with this type, whatever it may be; for it is certain that nobody has yet shown us its nature. What *exists* cannot be universal, in the Platonic sense of the word; and what is so universal cannot exist.

There are many other variations on the meaning of "universal" which I might adduce and all of which are incompatible with any actual form of Judaism. Of these I shall select one more—really a combination of the first two intentions with a third, that of supremacy or superiority. "Universal" is sometimes used as the equivalent of "dominant" or "prevailing." I have selected this meaning for final treatment because it represents the historical attitude toward the universality of Judaism, and the maximum fulness of its contemporary purport. This kind of universality is what the prophets hoped for and what our modern universalists feed their dreams with, consciously or unconsciously. The pax Romana, or the enforced catholicism of the Gregorian pontificate pretended to such a "universality." It does not mean the non-existence or impossibility of other religions, it means their subordination and repression. It does not mean the existence of Judaism as the *only* religion, for that would be destructive of Judaism as a *different* religion; it means the existence of Judaism as the dominating or supreme religion. This meaning of "universal" makes it synonymous with "imperialistic"; it assigns to Judaism an overruling position, such as it never yet had and is certain never to have. The notion of Judaism as the *only* religion identifies Judaism as religion, not as *a* religion, and hence abolishes the individuality of Judaism; and with its individuality, its supremacy. "Universal," in the sense of catholic, Judaism seeks nothing of the sort. It yearns for empire, not dissolution.

Consciously or unconsciously, for the most part unconsciously, this yearning is what keeps alive the idea, "universal." It is one phase or aspect of the sense of self in a more than a little psychopathic egotism which here manifests itself in its solidest as well as in its most insidious form. Its character and mechanics are, perhaps, nowhere so patent as in the history of religion. On the record, all religions are possessed of imperial ambitions. Their story is the story of unyielding attempts to *universalize* themselves by imposing themselves, by persuasion or by the sword, on all peoples. The God of Israel must needs conquer all other gods and rule in their place; the God of Christianity must supersede also the God of Israel as well as the popular gods; Mohammed's Allah must rule in the place of all three.

And, of course, the manifestation of God's rule comes

uniquely as the supremacy of his spokesmen and worshippers. The picture is of the continual pushing and pulling of this group of men or that to make all other groups agree with them about certain beliefs. And what were those beliefs particularly? They were beliefs in the modes, instruments and persons that had or have the supposititious power of securing their prosperity now or later. To challenge or to doubt these agencies, still seems to many people equal to challenging their personal right to live. So they seek agreement at any cost, nowadays, by means of missionaries, formerly by means of sectarian battles, excommunications, conversions, taboos, religious wars, inquisitions, etc. No enmity is so merciless as religious enmity, and the traces of this jealousy for one's pet instruments in preservation of self, transmitted for centuries, still, consciously or subconsciously, manifest their characteristic effects, even, if one is to judge from the newspapers, in the "universal" Jews of the Reformed Conference. But this intolerance of different things, which is a character-mark of all "universalizing" religions, is only the less harmful, spontaneous, coarser aspect of religious egotism. It is, all in all, normal and even healthy. Its other expression is much more dangerous because it assumes the most insidious of all pretenses—that of altruism. It is the lupine nature under the wool. It is the "mission of Israel," the mission to propagate "universal" Judaism. I shall say nothing of the obvious paradox of a "universal" doctrine requiring missionaries—the contradiction is too patent. I want in this regard to refer only to the personal attitude which I find underlying adherence to this contradiction.

That the "imperial" implications of "universal" must appeal to egotism is, I think, clear enough. The believer in a "universal" religion is endowed thereby with all the self-importance of the ancient Roman Senator. In some metaphysical, magical way, the thing he lives by is everywhere enforced, everywhere dominating, and what is most delightful, the subjects of its domination don't know it. He feels obliged to make them realize that only he is among the "elect"; only he and his kind are "chosen." And to what end? As Christians would say, to mediate between the damned and God and to save them in God's name. But intrinsically that is pretense, that is self-deluding rationalization. The fundamental motives of "missionaries" of any kind or sect is to strengthen themselves, not to improve others. It is their own peace of mind, salvation or glory, not the happiness of the converted they aim at. If our universalistic brethren aimed at the latter event, they would aim for the death of their religion and for the disappearance of their vocation. Their aim would be suicide. If everybody were converted, if everybody were to think as they and do as they, there would be no distinction between them and anybody else; their "priestly" function would be abolished, and their religion nullified as a thing to teach and preach. Judaism can be Judaism only insofar as it contains a differential which distinguishes it from other *isms* and rabbis rabbis only insofar as they can conserve that differential and communicate it to those who do not know it or cherish it.

Now our missionaries, so far as I can gather, recognize this, for they believe in the eternity of their "universal Judaism," in the eternity of their rabbinic function, etc. In fact, eternity is a characteristic of universality. One must conclude, then, that under the guise of "making the world better," they aim perhaps more genuinely at their own preservation and aggrandizement. The "mission of Israel" picks its adherent out of the crowd, sets him among the elect, makes him "bigger, better, and busier," gives him, in a word, imaginatively at least, that superior standing to which every man, even a layman, believes himself more entitled than his peers. And as in the Christian world in which Israel maintains itself, Israel has been forced into a status of inferiority, Israel must, of course, have a mission. Again the "universality" of Judaism gives its adherents the advantage of belonging to the majority—to the imagination, the "universal" is a *big* majority, being everywhere, at all times; has magical powers, etc. Its effect is imperial. If the "universalist" is not on top now, he inevitably will be later and the word of the Lord whose surrogate and spokesman he is will go forth from Cincinnati, if not from Zion.

This inmost vision of the self is the heart of "universalism." In business it makes trusts, in religion, catholics, in politics, empires. Of course, reformed Judaism must be "universal." How could a cult which signalizes itself as an endeavor to escape from the inferiorities and hardships of the ancestral position pretend to anything less? All evangelical or missionary religions have the same characteristic. Only the ancient paganisms and modern orthodoxies (insofar as these are still pagan), refuse to assert the obligation to proselytize and the attribute of universality, and hence can afford to let their gods live at least in armed truce, if not in neighborly peace with the gods of others. They are egotistic, no less so than the universalists, but they are content to live and to let live, to give and to take chances in the struggle for existence. They do not assert that nothing different may or shall be, that everything which differs must become the same as they. They only affirm that their right to be is not less than that of their alternatives and competitors, and they ask freedom in the exercise of that right. They are not compensating for inferior or insecure status with superior and imperial pretensions, unrealizable in fact and self-defeating as ideals. These pretensions are the whole import of "universal Judaism" as *this*, specific, religion; they mean an end to the religion of the Jews.

But Judaism is Judaism, not because it is merely religion, but because it is *a* religion, because it is different from Christianism or Mohammedanism or Vishnuism or Parseeism. Insofar as Judaism is religion only, it is nothing in particular. It begins to be an independent and identifiable faith only where it begins to be different from other faiths. Religions, like the men who make them, are real only insofar as they are different from other men, other religions, and other things; insofar as they are identical with other existences, i. e., "universal," they are negligible. If Dr. Kohler, of Cincinnati, is not at the very least *numerically* different from Dr. Foster, of Newark, how can even this minimal reality be credited to him? And he becomes progressively more his very interesting self, becomes progressively more real, as he reveals qualities which *distinguish* him from other people. But every such quality detracts from his universality and adds to his particularity. The more universal, the more insignificant he must be. The most universal thing in the world is "being." But who talks or deals with mere "being," even among philosophers? All their squabbles, like the squabbles of every man, concern this or that *particularity* of being. What woman loves "man" rather than *some* man? What pietist obeys "law" and not a law? Mere universals are empty, futile, impotent, nugatory. The law of gravitation never did anybody either harm or good; a particular falling stone, a concrete moving train, has infinite capacity for both. Particularity, as opposed to universality, is the essence of life and power. The most universal thing is the deadest.

To harp on the "universality" of Judaism, therefore, is

either to insist that it is futile, dead or moribund; or to give evidence of a state of mind which is the symptom of a fearful and defeated heart. Now, for the very obvious reason that Judaisms do exist and are engaged in a bitter struggle for survival with the world and with each other, the first alternative is inadmissible. The second, with all it implies of compensation for feelings of inferiority, is inevitable, especially when one considers that with the identification of "universal" Judaism as imperial, the highly interesting doctrine of the "mission of Israel" is closely connected. It is in this connection that we shall find the psychological cause of the apparent intellectual deficiency of our universalists, perhaps also some excuse for it and certainly the true indication of the concrete value of "universalism." I turn now, therefore, to a consideration of the psychological basis of the preference for the expression "universal."

II

There is in every language a large collection of terms which, because of their history, associations or purely accidental relationships, acquire an emotional coloring quite incommensurate with their signification and often quite opposed to the emotion that signification would of itself evoke. Such words are particularly imported into common usage from those disciplines that deal with the subtle and intangible parts of the environment—from theoretical physics, from theology, from philosophy, and even from psychology. The meanings of such words as "God," "Unity," "spirit," "science," "universal," "truth," "mental," etc., are appreciable by persons of a certain degree of training and technical equipment. To the man on the street they stand for no particular idea, and for no definite thing. They are significant of the profound, the mys-

terious and the magically powerful—they represent at
most an elusive potentiality for good and evil. They are
words of imminence,—*value-words;* that is, in the typical
mind they stand not for things, but for emotional attitudes. For example, people hate to be accused of materialism, or epicureanism, not because they *know* what the
words denote, but because they *feel* them as items of attack or insult, inferentially with meanings unpleasant and
dangerous. And they love to be called idealists, because
the word is felt as appreciative, as pleasant and creditable,
although, as a matter of fact, idealism may be psychologically and logically a very reprehensible and immoral
thing. The most obvious example among the religious cults
of our own time of the happy verbal combination of ir-
reconcilables is, of course, the expression "Christian Science," which actually denotes a thing which is neither
Christian nor scientific, and which could not be either or
both, for the reason that Christianity and science are abso-
lutely incompatible. At the same time Christian Scientists
are numerous; and most are such, not because they have
any idea of what the words in fact stand for, but because
the words in themselves have profound emotional force.
They are in common usage, primarily *value-words,* not
name words. To the feelings of the western world Christian
stands for one of the great historic concentrations of excellence inherited from the past. "Good" and "Christian"
are for many people interchangeable terms. So, again,
"science" stands for a new and more recent concentration
of value, and to as many other people "good" and "science"
are interchangeable. But the conflict of the two *things,*
Christianity and science, is also a matter of tradition and
inevitable regret, and *any* union of them is more desirable
than their separation. Therefore, when people hear the
phrase "Christian Science," they do not ask whether the

things have combined, they only *feel* the confluence of the emotional contexts of both words. Now emotional contexts of the same kind can and do combine, though the objects which evoke them frequently cannot and do not. I firmly believe that nine-tenths of the success of Mrs. Eddy's hysteric exudation rests upon its very clever name. Present the same shreds of doctrine by any other name and its lovers will shrink from it with terror and disgust. Attach but once thereto any word of great emotional connotation and the emotion suffuses and gives great value to most arrant nonsense. In fact, one can hear much "cultured" discourse among American women consisting of the repetition of such empty, but emotionally satisfying incantative formulae as "that blessed word, Mesopotamia."

Here, then, we have a first step toward an explanation of the persistence of that self-contradictory term, "universal Judaism." It is an expression like "Christian Science." It stands for two mutually exclusive things each of which by itself awakens pleasant feelings. The expression fuses the feelings without in any way influencing the things. "Universal" remains "universal" and "Judaism" remains "Judaism" but the feeling-tone of the two words spoken together is more than twice as nice as that of each spoken separately. So the feeling keeps the phrase current.

1910

IV

JUDAISM, HEBRAISM AND ZIONISM

In a discussion of the value of "universal" Judaism, printed some time ago in the AMERICAN HEBREW, I pointed out that logically, and therefore really, the term "universal Judaism" stands for repugnant and self-contradictory elements, and that its vogue was psychologically explicable by the fusion of the emotional states naturally relevant to each term, under the stress of that fundamental engine in human motive, egotism. I demonstrated, in brief, that "universal Judaism" stands for a private emotional condition, not for a publicly identifiable natural existent.

To this proposition the AMERICAN HEBREW has printed two rejoinders. One, by Mr. Max Raisin, announces that "Mr. Kallen honestly disclaims having any personal 'liking' for either Orthodoxy or Reform, or that *tertium quid* called conservative Judaism"—in other words . . . "he denies having anything in common with the Jews and Judaism of our day." And he invites Mr. Kallen "to have the fairness and the manliness to acknowledge that we who are not ashamed of belonging to either of the three contingents are not here out of sheer obstinacy and that we do not persist in Jewish separation simply and solely to remain a sect among sects."

The second reply is from the pen of Dr. Samuel Schulman who identifies himself as the aboriginal occasion of my analysis of "universal Judaism." His objection is like

Mr. Raisin's. "Judaism is a universal religion, to which Israel, a Priest-People, is bearing witness." My analysis of this universality is false because I am "a type of 'some intellectuals' who would have us commit ourselves to racialism or Zionism"; because I carry a "sneering question mark" on my face; because I am a Zionist for "biological reasons," which means "that the Jews should continue to live as a race though he deny everything Israel has stood for in history." Moreover, as I happen to be identified with that movement in modern thought known as pragmatism, I am told, *ex cathedra*, that "the consequences of my theory are such that they will destroy the Jews" and that hence my theory is false. "It's a particularly false thought in a very able mind whose conceit is sometimes somewhat cynical, but which does not hide the nakedness of the de-Judaised heart."

Now, both Messrs. Schulman and Raisin are guilty, to begin with, of an identical confusion of thought. Both imagine that the cogency of a discussion or the truth of a proposition is identical with the nature of its source. Hence their method is essentially an attempt to refute my argument by very courteous animadversions upon my person, my traits, and my incidental private beliefs, of which they are completely ignorant. All these may be of interest to the readers of the AMERICAN HEBREW, I dare say, but I submit that they are totally irrelevant to the question whether there is any such thing as "universal Judaism." Nor can I see how "fairness and manliness" are constituted by agreeing with Mr. Raisin, or how one is "de-Judaised" by disagreeing with Dr. Schulman. This business is so patently like "no brief, abuse the plaintiff's attorney," that it calls intrinsically for no reply whatever. But in the expression of their attitudes both Messrs. Raisin and Schulman have raised a certain new issue—

that of the function and destiny of the Jew. Each of these rabbis merely reasserts the dogma attacked. Mr. Schulman says: Judaism *is* universal and the Jews have the "mission of spreading or bearing witness to it." Mr. Raisin says, comically enough: The particular concreteness of Judaism consists in its universality and if it be not so, and the Jews have no mission, what justifies their separate existence? The answer to this question, is, after all, fundamental to the right conception of the status of Jewry, and I shall try to give what seems to me the correct account of this status and its implication. I shall therefore first speak of the implications of the "mission" of Jewry, then of the general moral sanctions for the persistence of any human group, and finally I shall inquire whether the Jews possess such sanctions.

I

The interesting thing about the assignation of a mission to Israel is the fact that, far from implying that the Jews actually have one, the assignation implies that the Jews have *not* a mission. People are bothered about their work or their destiny only when they are out of work and do not know what to do with their lives. The prophets had no conception of a "mission" of Israel; they conceived only of the imperial success of the Jewish nation, of Israel as the ruler, not the slave. The fanfaronade about the mission of Israel arose when the life of the Jewish people seemed most insecure and unjustified; it presupposes the anti-Semitic challenge of Jewry's right to that life. Nobody speaks of the "mission" of the English or of the Japanese, or of the Russians; nor is there a Japanese, or a Russian, or an English problem. "Mission" and "problem" are correlated terms in the history of Jewry. Human groups that are, as groups, normally and

vigorously functioning in civilization do not offer problems and do not proclaim missions. They are accepted at
their face value, they need no excuse for their existence;
their mere being and doing what they are and do is their
"mission." There is nothing in the life of the Russians or
Japanese or English that constitutes a "problem" as the
total life of any Jewish group constitutes a "problem";
and what is that problem if not the very particular and
concrete situation of contemporary Jewry—a situation
essentially pure maladjustment, a thing out of gear and
going wrong? A situation and not a theory, something the
matter *here* and *now*, not in the past or the future; a
situation identical, in a word, with just that status of
Jewry which Dr. Samuel Schulman elects to praise as
"international Judaism"? The Jewish problem is nothing
if it is not exactly that actual condition of the Jewish
people which the early reforming Jews of Germany felt
so painfully that they devised as a charm against it, the
notion that the Jews are a "priest-people" and that Israel
has a "mission." If there had been no problem, if these
men had not observed that among human groups in the
western world, Israel alone was allotted no positive virtues, that Israel alone was required to provide an excuse for
existing, Israel would never have been endowed with a
"mission." And this "mission," be it observed, though
without a doubt a source of personal comfort and cosmic greatness to Dr. Schulman and his kind, is not a solution of the Jewish problem in any sense whatever of the
word solution. On the contrary, it is the assertion that the
Jewish problem has no solution. It is to say that the
Jewish problem is its own justification.

Such, then, is the logical implication of the "mission"
of the Jews. It is an instruction to Jewry to be damned
for the glory of God. But, significantly, those who issue

this instruction are comfortably cushioned in America and England, they are not among the damned of Russia's Kishineff and Kieff or Rumania's Bucharest. Their advice, moreover, gives the lie to the character assigned to the historical God of Israel, who may be jealous and punitive, but whose intention has always been described as looking toward the national competence and imperial majesty of Israel, toward the well-being of His chosen. And such an intention is not compatible with the eternal persistence of a "Jewish question." However, be the theological aspect of this contradiction what it may—morally, "problem," difficulty, disharmony, maladjustment, no matter how caused, can have no justification whatever. Morally, if the situation of the Jews constitutes a "question," the only possible *right* action is *to change the situation*.

Now change in a social as in any other situation may be achieved in two ways. One of the ways is to eliminate altogether the lesser element of the conflict. The other is to redistribute, to separate these discrepant elements. The Jews have actually just two alternatives before them. On the one hand, they may be eliminated by violent and speedy destruction or by slower absorption into the neighboring peoples, by assimilation. On the other hand, a remnant may be gathered from the four corners of the earth and renationalized, may reconstitute the Jewish polity in Palestine or elsewhere.

Of these alternatives I choose the latter. As Dr. Schulman has already been good enough to proclaim for the purpose of exhibiting my degraded state and my shame, I am a Zionist. I look toward the concentration and renationalization of the Jews. I am committed to the persistence of a "Jewish separation" that shall be national, positive, dynamic and adequate. And Mr. Raisin very properly inquires, to what end, if the Jews have no mission? What justifies the separate national existence of the Jews?

To answer this question it is necessary to indicate certain fundamental ethical principles that may be discovered in the estimates of all nations alike. If the Jews express these principles, they are morally entitled to continued existence, not otherwise.

II

We have seen that the present situation of the Jews, in whatever region of the civilized world you will, constitutes a problem. Any relief offered presupposes another problem, which is fundamental and lies behind this one— the moral problem, the problem of values. In essence, the "Jewish question" is an ethical disharmony. Its solution demands the testing of the Jews in the light of certain *natural* standards and unchallengeable natural ideals of conduct among nations. It raises the issue of international policy; it requires the envisagement of the inevitable natural form of international life; it requires the analysis of the relation of the Jews thereto.

The form is not far to seek. It springs from the nature of human life itself. Any moment of existence is a more or less perfect embodiment of it. Its essence is the identity and coalescence of instrument with purpose, service with self-preservation, means with end, use with self-expression. Since Aristotle men have been wont, rightly, to distinguish two kinds of goodness; first, the goodness of the instrument, goodness *for* something else, as a knife is good for cutting bread, and bread for supporting life; and then, intrinsic goodness, goodness in itself, not for anything extraneous. It is peculiar that intrinsic goodness is the stopping-place; it is the goal of service, it justifies the instrument, it is presupposed in the very existence of instruments, but in itself has no purpose and serves no end. Intrinsic goodness is its own justification, i.e., it has no justification. All things in the world, from microbes to trusts, are good in and for themselves; their evil is purely instrumental, their evil is their *effect* on other things which have the same freehold in that struggle of interests which we call society.

Morally, the great intrinsic excellence is life. The whole machinery of society—government, art, commerce, religion—have arisen and maintain themselves as instruments or methods in the conservation and improvement of life. They are justified in so far as they secure this end, immoral if they fail to do so. Life is the culmination, the absorption, the very nature and seat of value. Our customs and conventions, our laws and traditions, therefore, condone various anti-social acts when performed in defense and preservation of life and condemn even social acts which result in the loss or destruction of life. Self-defense is the right excuse for homicide, but the murder of even a source of evil is punishable by death.

Now as there is more than one kind of social life, as men live first as members of groups, and again as individuals, it is inevitable that lives shall conflict with and destroy each other or shall harmonize, shall be instrumental to each other as an incident in the business of preserving each itself. There is fundamentally a struggle for survival in which the *intrinsic* goodness of the units is never moral unless it happens at the same time to be good *instrumentally*. An instance may make this point clearer. Suppose that in one family there are two sons, one with a natural talent for fiddling, a musician by birth, the other with a natural talent for stealing, a congenital thief. The whole life, the whole individuality of the fiddler will be concentrated in his development as a fiddler. He is more completely himself, more completely self-justified, the better he plays, the more efficiently he understands and exercises his art. But fiddling happens also to be an instrumental, a social good. The fiddler has no "mission" to fiddle, he is no more responsible for his nature than is the perfect frog or the lily in the field; his happiness lies in being most completely and adequately a musician in the perfect exercise of his natural function of fiddling. He fiddles by instinct, and because this happens incidentally to be also a social service, of use to others, these others protect, reward and honor him. In him happiness and service, instrument and end are identified. In his brother, the thief, on the contrary, there is no such identification. The thief's happiness, like the fiddler's, would lie in the development and perfection of his natural function; he would be most truly himself the better he snatched purses, broke safes, robbed houses. But good as this thief's life might be in and for it itself, it is *instrumentally* anti-social, and society tries to get rid of burglars. The social complex can cohere mainly as the equilibrium of different interests sustained by the coalescence of instrumental with intrinsic goodness.

This being the inevitable moral situation, it follows that the mere existence, the mere "being there" of any individual or group, though good in and for itself, is no ground whatever for the continuance of that existence. And it follows that every concurrent motive, like pity, philanthropy, religion, dislike of suffering, which might move people to help the already existing to go on doing so, may be even more immoral than that existence itself, since the motive aids and abets what is useless and noxious. The conservation of no social object whatever is morally justified unless it is an actual synthesis of instrument and end, unless by *being most itself, by making the most of its individuality,* by perfecting itself in its natural function, it most avails the rest of mankind.

Races and nations are somewhat less amenable to this ideal than are individuals. The morality of groups is like the group-mind, a very much cruder and coarser thing than that of individuals. Comity among the nations is less orderly and integrative; self-preservation is still profoundly anti-social; the great political activities are land-grabbing, armament-construction, commercial exploitation, tariff-wars. International life is still much a life of cross-purposes, conflict and destruction. The tariff madness is perhaps the best example of this condition. Whereas under universal free trade each nation would be freely exercising its natural productive function to the uttermost, would be perfecting itself and benefiting the rest, under the tariff system production conflicts with production, economic life is a deformity and a menace to the state's safety, tearing it up and disintegrating it from within and creating enemies without. On the other hand, in the more truly significant forms of international life, in those forms that constitute culture, comity and co-operation are direct and inevitable. In the policing of the high seas and the suppression of piracy, of slavery, of disease, in the perfection and interpretation of literature, of art, of the sciences and cultures, instrument and end coalesce; all nations are working together, each in its unique way, to perfect itself and to preserve and enrich the whole.

The outcome of these *non-destructive, self-expressive* activities of nations is that fulness and richness of human affairs the material of which we name civilization, the spirit of which we designate as culture. They are industry, commerce, government, religion, art, literature, science and philosophy, arising as the unique actual functions of especial human groups and polities, arising as continuations and fulfilment of the past racial tradition and inheritance. Culture thus constitutes a harmony, of which peoples and nations are the producing instruments, to which each contributes its unique tone, in which the whole human past is present as an enduring tension, as a background from which the present comes to light and draws its character, color, vitality. It is this culture, so conceived, which is the standard whereby any nation or race is judged for conservation or destruction. A human group is moral, socially valuable, entitled to continued life, only in so far as it has a distinct nature that produces an individual note, a note that enriches and changes the harmony, not a mere overtone, a secondary and derivative thing, but a thing primary, fundamental, tonic.

The Jews, in the degree that they are a differentiated and distinct human group, on whatever basis, racial or sectarian, are morally entitled to life only if that difference is elementally and by its very nature contributory to the values of culture and civilization. If of themselves they constitute a problem, if by nature they cause discord, they are condemned. To demonstrate their ethical right to be is to demonstrate that "the Jewish problem" is incidental and unnecessary, that the real effect of the Jews is a positive and constructive effect, that by remaining their living selves, by perfecting their natural and distinctive group functions they must contribute to the welfare of nations and serve international comity.

III

Do and can the Jews fulfil these conditions? For answer one must turn to history and ethnology, to the discussion of many recondite and vexed questions that re-

quire much detail and are difficult of popular formulation.
If what I say runs contrary to accepted opinion and traditional belief, it is because I have studied these matters
in order to find the truth, not to apologize for the Jew.
Among other things it is what I found in history and ethnology that made a Zionist of me. The difference between
what seems to me the truth about the history and ethnology of the Jews and the traditional account, requires,
I know, considerable elucidation, but I cannot here undertake more than to suggest the barest outlines of such a
discussion.

Historically, the basis of culture has always been ethnic
and geographically political. Groups have not been active
functional units in civilization where they have lacked
predominant social tradition or have not been, *en masse,*
geographically distinct political units. That the Jews, in
classic times, have had these properties I need not argue.
That they now have racial unity is properly enough dis-
puted; that they have nationality the "diaspora" would
seem to preclude. As the only evidence and guarantee for
the future efficacy of the Jews as a group must be their
past, their history, the positive justification for Zionism
must be sought in the history of the Jews; it must bring
the fact of social inheritance and of geographico-political
individuality clearly to light.

In history the culture of the Jews appears as no mere
religion; in the world's count of it, it receives another
name and a different estimate. It is called Hebraism, not
Judaism, and to be a lover of Hebraism is more than to be
a Judaist. A sectarian life, as Mr. Raisin very properly
suggests, is no excuse whatever for separation. Sects and
dogmas pass, ethnic groups and cultures endure. The
blindness and insensibility of "reform" lies in the failure
or refusal to recognize this fact and in the consequent

attempt to thin the richness of Jewish existence to the verbal tenuousness of a few unproved dogmas and to substitute for concrete Jewish living the anatomical horror of their "Jewish science." Hebraism is a life and not a tradition; Judaism is a spirit, a concrete and particular mode of behavior, not a formula. They are growing and changing things, expressions of a palpable vitality, not dead unalterable "universals." The true deniers of "everything Israel has stood for in history," are those alone who would substitute the bloodless "universal" for the fecund concrete life. What really destroys the Jews is what "universalizes" them, what empties their life of distinctive particular content and substitutes void phrases to be filled with any meaning the social and religious fashion of the day casts up. Hebraism, what "Israel has stood for in history," is the life of the Jews, their unique achievement,—not as isolated individuals, but as a well-defined ethnic group,—in government, in industry and commerce, in social economy, in the arts, in religion, in philosophy. Hebraism is the particular inheritance of the Jews, their tradition and their culture, potently efficacious in contemporary Jewish living, its matrix and inspiration.

The historic content of Hebraism was in metaphysics the vision of reality in flux; in morals, the conception of the value of the individual, in religion, the conception of Yahweh as a moral arbiter. That the national life in Palestine, expressed in the Scriptures, is the source of a considerable portion of the moral and religious ideas of the western world is, of course, a commonplace. What is not so clearly apprehended is the fact that the Jews, as an *ethnic group*, were the great middlemen of mediaeval times, and that what they disseminated was as much the wisdom of the ancients as the commodities of commerce. Related only in the most incidental fashion to the polities of Europe, they lived an organic, inner political life of their own, distinct and segregated from all others, and as its social expression, generated the basis of the present efficacious financial system, helped preserve and restore the ancient wisdom to Europe and practiced with signal distinction the art of medicine. In modern times the life of the majority of the Jews has been no less national, confined as they are to the pales of settlement, though it has been less obviously contributory to civilization—the emphasis appearing to lie on the notion of political and economic freedom. To culture Jewry has contributed a significant bi-lingual literature, Hebrew and Yiddish, just as the earlier ages saw the creation of Talmudic and Hebrew. From Amos to Karl Marx and from the singer of Deborah's song to Perez, the vision of the world and the expression of life has been continuous yet varying for the Jews and honestly efficacious for western civilization.

That this vision and expression are rooted in ethnic solidarity and a geographical concentration, practically equivalent to nationality, any one with eyes may see. The isolation of the Jews is traditional, but the notion of the "diaspora" as *absence from Palestine* has taken such hold of the world's imagination that the life of the Jewish mass as *presence in another region* was not thought of, the various devices that, during the Middle Ages, made a federated European Jewry were not considered. As a matter of fact, the "diaspora" is only a partial thing; it is like the diaspora of the English in the British Empire. The Jews always had a center of reference, a spiritual capital to look to; in the long run the *majority* of them have throughout their history lived together and lived a homogeneous national life.

In sum: Up to within a century ago the Jews of the world as a *majority,* lived an organic social life and have expressed it in a culture which has been continually efficacious in the wider world. The "Jewish problem," for the Jews the problem of the Jewish spirit, began with the external and artificial attempt to thin Hebraism down to a mere sectarian Judaism. There is every reason to believe this attempt, however well intended, dangerous to Jewish survival. On the record, Reform has tended not toward the purification of religion, but toward its nullification. True reform moves from within, not without. It is a growth, not a surgical operation. The masses of Jewry are untouched by reformed Judaism; the classes are alienated by it from Jewry. Reformed Judaism appears to have cut itself off from the sources of its own life. These sources are the Jewish nationality. There is no intrinsic quarrel—in spite of hysterical Zionists and rabid reformers—between reformed Judaism and Zionism. Jewish religion is a function and an expression of nationality and depends on nationality for life. Dr. Schechter has already pointed this out clearly enough. If Messrs. Schulman and Raisin honestly care about preserving Judaism, they can do so only by co-ordinating it to that larger flowering of the Jewish spirit which we call Hebraism, a flower whose roots are nationality and whose soil is culture. Zionism is the solution of the Jewish problem because, if the past is any warrant for the future, there is every reason to believe that with the Jews as a free people in Palestine or elsewhere, that unique note which is designated in Hebraism has a chance to assume a more sustained, a clearer and truer tone in the concert of human cultures, and may genuinely enrich the harmony of civilization.

1910

V

JUDAISM AND THE MODERN POINT OF VIEW

The religious temper of the 19th century was one of peculiar instability and uncertainty. It was marked in alternation by hysterical assertiveness, by believing timidity, by obstinate dogmatism, and by a tolerant scepticism which set its hope in works rather than in faith. The fact is that although religion was subject to the same rapid changes of fortune as the other European institutions, it was far more than they exposed to disaster in these changes. Winds of doctrine blew in on it from every human source. They blew in from the social and political ideas which underlay the French Revolution and the subsequent spread of democratic government. They blew in from the economic theories which underlay and expressed the stupendous change initiated by the use of machinery, which we now call industrialism. They blew in from the pathetic sentimentalism in the fine arts that generated the romantic movement with pre-Raphaelitism and its mid-Victorian rococo. They blew in from that overwhelming accumulation of positive knowledge which we call science. The winds from that quarter were particularly strong. They overturned altogether at its very foundations the generating assumptions of theology. They swept in and deposited that method of analysis and exegesis which is called, rather ridiculously, "higher criticism." They pounded revelation with archaeology and dialectic with fact. From the biological sciences, the winds were especially gusty; the bitter controversies over "evolution" and the "descent of man" are still within the memory of the present generation, and the rigorous and thoroughgoing logical demolitions of the Darwinian hypotheses are still to be had in the libraries.

Sole objective of such blasts as these, it is no matter of surprise that theology and even the religious sentiment were shaken and reduced from dogmatism to fideism. Religion, only a century before the age-long and secure measure of everything else, found itself in need of self-justification, of demonstrating its place and right in human life and civilized society. It began to exhibit itself as the defender of morals, as the guide of man through animal darkness which alone its light of fear could dispel, as the conservator of failing virtue and the sustainer of courage in a world which without it would have been an anarchic hell. Or again, it sulked and feared and withdrew from the field of life. In John Henry Newman, to cite a typical case, and the Oxford movement, it reasserted the salvational power of the old orthodoxies; and, as the weak and fearful mind, distraught by the complexity of its own creations and achievements had done once before, committed its destinies to the *credo quia impossibile*. Such ascetic withdrawal was, however, only sporadic. In the Protestant mass, religion, after an intense, though brief and not too hysterical struggle, capitulated and blew as the winds of doctrine listed. The supernatural destiny of the soul ceased to be its theme. The dogmas of revelation ceased to be its criteria. These became symbols only, and of the *new* view. For in order to conserve itself, religion made alliance with the *new* forces that are the essence of our modern world. Its other-worldliness has given way to a worldliness in which piety, in the last decade of the nineteenth century, becomes identical with humanitarian passion; in which salvation is no longer postponed to a region translunar and is announced to be earthly, practical, and immediate. Empirically, the religious temper of the age proclaims that the kingdom of God is to be here and now, that its content is social justice, that its creator and sustainer is Man as much as God. Metaphysically and theologically, religion has been through that decade, modest and humble. It offered instead of dogma, the subdued "I believe such and such about God's nature and will, and if I am wrong I can't lose anything and if I am right, think of my infinite gain!" It no longer repeated its arrogant "I know God's word and will."

II

This state did not last however. Though, up to date, the socialization of the religious sentiment has been practically unrestrained, so that men are less and less concerned about the salvation of their own souls and more and more about the betterment of society; though religious sentiment throughout the western world tends to be predominantly "prophetic," it has quickly lost its new modesty and has withdrawn its concessions to science and the scepticism of science. "I know" is again beginning to take back its place from "I believe." The reason lies in the history of science itself. Scientists, in all fields of their endeavor save perhaps mathematics and psychology, found themselves stumped by a number of problems. In the face of this stump their 19th century optimism broke down. They became in their turn uncertain and fearful of their methods. They began to investigate these methods, by which they had sworn. "Aha," they said, "here's the trouble. We are after all men trying to get on in a world which wasn't made for us. Our scientific methods are only tools, only crutches and stilts that help us through this world. They are instruments of control, not of revelation, 'methodological postulates,' 'scientific fictions,' and they serve us only practically, not theoretically. We can't *know* anything by means of them. *Ignoramus, ignorabimus.* Agnosticism is the only destiny of man's knowledge."

But man is not content with agnosticism. If science and the intellect can't know, then religion and the heart *must.* Romanticism and sentimentalism, hence, have always insisted on a way of knowing which is superior to that of science. That way is revelation, intuition. The discomfort of science is for this reason the hope of theology. Sentimentalism announces that intuition reveals what science falsifies. In it spirit is restored to the mastery of the world, man's assurances of immortality are renewed, and his ultimate victory over evil is secured. All this, science has denied him; all this, intuition offers him. So Bergson and Eucken assure him, and they are experts in philosophic intuition. And on the basis of this assurance theological dogmatism raises its head once more. But the dogmatism is not the ancient formal one. It is modified by all the traits which the religious sentiment acquired during the 19th century. Consequently, the most frequent word in all the reaches of contemporary Christianity is the word *new.* We are told of the "new" theology; the "new" catholicism, the "new" this and that. While the orthodox word of reproach is "modern." Modernism, the Pope writes in the encyclical "Pascendi Gregio," is the synthesis of all the heresies. It consists, however, in nothing more than the use of "higher criticism," immediate moralism, and Darwinian utilitarian standards as the methods, criteria and sanctions of theology. The novelty consists in nothing more than in refusing to localize and in refusing to specify the nature of that force and go in the constitution of the world and in the history of man, as science does; in calling it the real and true which only intuition reveals and in applying to it the terms of "God" and "grace." Furthermore, it abolishes the ancient conflict between science and religion *ex cathedra*. Harmony and only harmony, the "new" and modernist theology asserts, can exist between science and religion. For religion is the human spirit perceiving absolute truth, and science is merely the instrument of that spirit in getting about the world. Science hence may say anything, for it is not authoritative. Only religion can know.

Is it too much to say that in this adventurous history European Christianism has been moving to that quality of temper and tendency which is characteristic of Judaism? I am not sure. If Judaism were the simple phenomenon some of its apologists of the "reform" sect would make it out to be, the answer would be easily, No.

But Judaism, more than any other western religion, is a corporate thing, woven inextricably into the texture of the people's life whence it springs. And when taken so, the answer seems to me to be, Yes.

This does not mean that Judaism possesses all truth once and for all. The answer is No, because Judaism, corporately taken, does not assume to possess all truth once and for all. Like any other religion it has a history, and during the 19th century, as adventurous a history as any. Adherents of the reform sects are apt to boast of the modernism of the changes which their sect stands for, to describe them as adjustments of Judaism to modern conditions of life and thought. Adherents of the orthodox sects, the Mizrachist, and the youthful sentimentalists who think to find a "new" realm of grace by restoring an old ritual, have also their own pride and their own boasts. Judaism, in a word, exhibits all the marks of having undergone the passion of the 19th century. Yet, corporately, as the religion of a people, it seems to me to have assimilated more and to have been transformed less than other western religions. I do not discover a "new" theology in Judaism, nor a "new" moralism, nor a particularly latter-day modernity. (I am of course speaking of the religion of *Kelal Israel,* not of the theological fashions of a school or a sect.) Judaism seems to have contained some labile principle which makes its basic teaching far less needy of revision than other religions. Baldly, this principle may be indicated by the words *naturalism* and *moralism*. These qualities make Jewish religion compatible with any phase of science and accommodating to every pressing human need.

III

Let me, before elaborating this proposition, make clear that I do not mean by Judaism any particular theological dogma or system of dogmas. These are invariably the last terms and surfaces of a developing insight, and no more reveal what lies underneath than does an animal's skin. In the second place, and for the same reason, I do not mean by Judaism any particular ritual or body of ritual. While these are more significant and expressive than dogmas, for they represent the active relationship between a people and its putative supernatural fellowship, they tend too easily to become mechanized and rigid and to become emptied of meaning. Thus the practices of tearing open the wall of the synagogue, of measuring graves with candles, and so on, in sanitary and other crises, may be ritually much more significant of the living religious activities of the Jews than the ritual of the Alioth. As a ritual Judaism must be held to comprise all practices of which Jewish groups avail themselves to bring them into dynamic relations with their God. As a theology, Judaism must be held to comprise all opinions that ever were *efficacious* in Jewish groups concerning the nature of this God and his relation to man. Judaism, hence, if it is to be understood impartially and objectively, must be understood as literally a complex phase of the *life* of the Jewish people.

It must not, however, be taken as the whole of that life. There are great regions of it which are turned in quite other directions than God. The whole of the life of the Jews, in all its phases, is best designated as Hebraism, and Judaism is best understood as a special aspect of this Hebraism, the aspect, namely, which comprises the sentiments, theories, doctrines and practices which relate to God. That, as compared with the religions of other westerners, Judaism is overwhelmingly integrative and comprehensive, often penetrating through and through the life of the masses, I not only grant but assert. Nevertheless, it is not identical with the whole of that life, and hence not the adequate expression of the spirit of the Jews, which is Hebraism. I have argued this point elsewhere and will say no more about it here. I wish to insist simply on this: that if Judaism be taken as it must be taken, scientifically, viz: as that body of sentiments, opinions, doctrines and practices expressing through history the efficacious attitude of the Jews as a whole toward God, then Judaism, revealed and dogmatic religion though it claims to be, has remained more constant, more adaptable and more progressive than other European religions. This, because, let me repeat, Judaism seems to have been naturalistic and realistic, while other religions have been supernaturalistic and salvational. As religious "progress" in the 19th century consisted in the naturalization and socialization of religious sentiment and doctrine, contemporary religious opinion, among both Protestants and Catholics, is reaching the logical and sentimental status which has long been that of Judaism.

IV

To begin with the naturalism. The essence of naturalism is the hypothesis that underneath and above the definite data of experience and thought, the whole march and panorama of nature, and the stream of our daily life, is a stuff which is their very force and go, their life. With regard to any one of these, this stuff is indifferent. Its laws generate for them both good *and* evil, and their destiny consists in so conforming to these laws as to gain the good and escape the evil. Naturalism says nothing concerning the nature of this dominant stuff; it may be "spirit," it may be "matter." Naturalism does not know. It knows only that every particular one of the stuff's manifestations is incommensurate with its totality, but that each, when studied positively and directly, reveals its force and tendency, and that the knowledge of this force and tendency composes its laws. The laws serve as practical guides to the mind in its adaptation to the world.

The resemblance between this and what is dominant in historic Judaism is striking. Yahweh has no specific image. His closest integrate definition is the extraordinary and much sermonized "I am that I am." Yet his manifestations are utterly naturalistic and empirical. He shows himself as fire, as thundercloud, as storm, as the creator of monsters, as a man, and so on. In many of the psalms,* as in the profoundest Biblical text which has survived, in Job, he is represented (by both Job and his friends) as taking all shapes from Ma to Mahi, that change and perish all, while he remains. He is represented as dealing out indif-

* Notably Psalm 78.

ferently good and evil, as having that absolute justice of indifference, of working out his purposes without reference to any of his particular creatures—simply the impartial *life* of all of them. God, according to the Book of Job, is his manifestations, both immanent and transcendent, different from them all as the whole is different from the part, but not otherwise; not different, as in the supernatural conceptions of him, by *existing apart*. It is only under Hellenistic and anthropomorphizing influences that this notion came to dominate Judaism, and it was never a congenial or governing one.

The knowledge of God and his laws, again, was to be attained *empirically and directly,* by no intermediaries, through a study of his manifestations. As Jehudah Halevi insists again and again: at Sinai God was immediately manifest to all the people, and his Torah is only the form of this natural manifestation. Descriptions of his character and desires consequently will vary with the occasion. They will always be empirical and often contradictory, for the *whole* pursues all purposes indifferently and contradiction is characteristic only of the view of the part. In rabbinic theology (and rabbinic theology is here most representative, for it incarnates the *effective* doctrines of Judaism, those that were being used and questioned, not academically, but in the very life of the people) the contradictions are as numerous as they are manifest. God is both personal and impersonal, anthropomorphic and unknowable, in the world and out of it, the source of goodness and the source of evil—all things, like and unlike, that have force and are efficacious influences on the problem in hand and on its favorable solution. The one quality that seems to remain the same in all these conflicting descriptions is this *efficacy, energy, life,* which the conflicting things have. This, indeed, goes so far, that the Torah, in

Hellenizing theology identified with Eternal Wisdom, with the Logos or mind of God, is in the life of the people but the potency of history. Even the Torah *changes*. Its words are fruitful and multiply. It consists not of the scriptures merely, but of the prophets, the hagiographa, *the whole recorded life* of the Jewish people—in a word, of the wisdom gleaned through experience with the world.

I have said in this no word about the so-called "unity" of God. But a great deal of twaddle has been written about it by the "reform" sect and there has been a tendency to impute to a dogma of "pure monotheism," a sort of magical power. Now, metaphysically and logically, there is no greater advantage, whether of purity or any other sort, in a monotheism than in a polytheism or trinitarianism. If the monotheism is taken to mean that only *one* supernatural spirit exists, Judaism is not monotheistic, for it patently entertained hordes of angels and demons and knew it. If the monotheism is taken to mean that only one supreme or ruling being exists, that the universe is a monarchy, then Judaism is not different from the religion of the Greeks or any religion which adores a pantheon with an overruling god. Logically, to say that God is one, is tautology, for any subject of discourse must be to that extent one, if it is to be spoken of at all. The "unity" of God, hence, can have meaning only if God is supposed to be divided against himself. We do not defend the "unity" of anything unless it is menaced. In point of fact, the common religious sense of the Jewish people has been far truer to the right meaning of the formula in the *Shemang* from which the doctrine of "unity" derives, than the uncommonly stupid dialectic of the theologians. We should simply be amused by a group of Democrats who intoned "Hear, O Americans, the President of the United States is One," yet we solemnly and ridiculously

continue to repeat the "Hear, O Israel, Yahweh our God is
One!"

Now, if we had been less anxious to reform and more
willing to know and to understand, we should have seen
that the *Shemang* by its very phrasing implies a contrast
and an assertion of superiority on behalf of Israel's God.
Its meaning must be rather: Yahweh our God alone is
God, or Yahweh our God is the only God, and it is this
meaning that seems to have been the socially effective one.
It takes the "unity" of God for granted, but it takes his
diversity for granted, too. In the Judaic tradition, not the
sporadic theological system, both are on the same level.
God is held to be, as in Job and the Psalms, no less than
by the rabbis, *identical with his manifestations*. He is
practically not one, but many-in-one, with the manyness
just as real as the oneness—often, indeed, more so, for
it is the particularity, the special quality of his manifestation, not his mere being, that counts practically.* If God
is one, then he is one as a man is one, from childhood to
death. He is one in the *continuity and development* of his
manifestations, one *dynamically* and *historically*. Each
year of life is different from the other, each natural fact is
different from the other, yet one passes into the other in
such wise that the child is the "same" person as the man,
that the force is the "same" force in heat, electricity,
gravitation. This oneness is the oneness that science sees.
It is on exactly the same level with the manyness, and it
is *temporalistic, active, creative,* a unity of history, not of
stuff. Existence, hence, for man and God, is an evolution,
a *dramatic development* of both man and God in which
all things change, nothing is immutable, not even the de-
crees of the Torah. That, we have seen, is regarded by the
rabbis as a *growing* thing, and may itself be abrogated in

* Cf. Schechter: Some Aspects of Rabbinic Theology, Chapter II.

behalf of *mercy*. Consequently, the religious *life* of the people is not static, it is itself an evolution, and an enrichment of tradition with losses as well as gains.

V

Thus far there is no conflict between Judaism as a theory and practice of life and any or all of the phases of positive science. There exists, it is true, a social organization among the Jews which the reform sect regards as antiquated. But its governing principle is not antiquated, and it was recognized by none so well as by the rabbis who, as *censores morum*, had authority in these things, that they are historic growths and not eternal laws, that they are consequently subject to constant revision. But this revision must turn on *a change within*, not an excision from without, on "evolution" rather than "revolution." The reform sects have been too sudden to be significant, their principles and views consequently have left the life of the great Jewish masses untouched. They belong to a class, not to a people. Yet, so-called orthodoxy has been far from standing still during the 19th century. And orthodoxy is a way of life, not a collection of eviscerated doctrine and apologetic. That it is suffused with much superstition and nonsense is, of course, true. But nobody who knows anything about the nature and history of religions will select that for special condemnation. The significant thing is that nowhere else in western religions are the superstition and nonsense so little capable of withstanding science and sense. These penetrate with extraordinary ease into the very ritual and corporate life of the Jewish masses. The reason is that Judaism is so largely and literally a *mode of life*. And the principle of life is *change*, and change for the sake of life. From this it is that the other generic quality of Judaism, its *moralism*, derives.

The union of *naturalism* with *moralism* is philosophically the most extraordinary quality a religion can possess. All other moralistic religions are *supernatural*. They regard the world as divinely governed, but governed from without, so that they require to divide their universe into two realms—a realm of grace and a realm of nature. Existence in the realm of nature presupposed a degradation, a fall from perfection, original sin, the total depravity of man. The business of life, hence, is to escape from sinful existence in nature to a sinless existence beyond nature, in grace. Each man must abandon family, society, all the world, and seek to save his own soul. His life must have an other-worldly aim; his goal must be *salvation*. His virtues on earth, consequently, must be negative virtues, as Macchiavelli says, virtues of suffering, not virtues of performance. His strength is a strength to *endure*, not a strength to do, and the world, hence, is given over into the hands of the wicked.

For Judaism, however, existence, life, is a good here and now. There is no original sin, there is no fall. The rewards and punishments of conduct are here and now woven into the warp and woof of nature herself. *The moral order is not a supernatural order, the moral order is a natural order.* Incommensurate though God and man are, there is a directive preference *in* the universe, a "something not ourselves which makes for righteousness," which we feel and can obey, and must obey if we desire prosperity, and length of days. Whatever man's aim, man's *business* is not salvation; man's business is *righteousness*—"to do justice, and love mercy, and walk humbly with thy Lord." Life on earth is not something to escape from. Life on earth is something to enjoy. It is obedience to the law, of course, but the law is not negative. The law is positive. It enjoins action, not abstinence, and this action is never private, it is *social*. It is something demanded by one's determinate relation to one's fellows. There is a pervasive good and evil, the so-called merit (*Zechuth*) and demerit, of ancestry, of offspring, of neighbors. The social consequences of every individual's act flow in all directions. Morality is corporate and rests on individual responsibility.

Consequently, there is no minutia of conduct which is without some social significance and cosmic bearing, and which must not be estimated by these. Such estimation requires their constant readjustment to novelty of situation, individual case, and corporate standard. This readjustment used to be the special business of the rabbis, and people who are impatient of discipline and without social perception call it "legalism." But if so, all truly integrated ethical living is legalistic. For society grows and fructifies by the interpretation of law in such wise as to harmonize it with new situations, and the adequacy of the social sense of a people may be measured by its "legal" tradition. "Legalism" means that Judaism could be and is progressive, that it contains the principle of growth within itself.

What is "legalism" in detail is "moralism" in the mass. And because *moralism* is positive, social and active, as opposed to *salvationism*, which is negative, private and passive, Judaism carries with it a joy of life that the rabbis called the "joy of the law." Judaism, consequently, as a corporate ethical tradition, has no conflict with the vision of human life enjoined by science. And this vision, essentially so Judaistic, contemporary non-Judaistic religious sentiment is now discovering and making its own. With a difference, however. The other-worldly, supernaturalistic bias remains fundamental. It has been moved from heaven *into* the world, but, we have Eucken's word for it, it is not *of* the world. Morality and the satisfaction of human hopes are still facts of grace, resting on a profounder level than the facts of nature. They are eternal, nature is in flux; nature derives from them. For Judaism, however, morality and things of the spirit are natural facts to be empirically described and understood. It requires no miracle to exhibit the moralism of the universe, creative, infinite, inscrutable though it be. Man knows it immediately, as we are told in Job, and verifies his knowledge pragmatically. Nature and spirit, hence, are not alien, they are one, and the science that describes the one characterizes the other. Even though Judaism is a revealed religion and thus in logic and method alien to the scientific point of view, what it reveals is itself so indeterminate, so much the essence of change, that it remains, I think, truer to the spirit of positive knowledge and possesses consequently a greater capacity for endurance and for growth.

But maybe not. For living Judaism is, after all, the thoughts of living Jews about themselves, their brethren, their neighbors and their life and destiny in the world. As Jews think, so Judaism is. . . .

1911

VI

A CONVERT IN ZION

We were five around a table. Our discussion had become very lively and its tone depressed, because, as is usual wherever thoughtful Jews gather to talk, we had drifted from the weather, the stage and the war to the Jewish Question, and on that topic we had stayed, in a deepening gloom. Cohen, who is a rabbi, but is genuinely religious, had saddened us with a portrayal of the defection of the young from the synagogue—orthodox and reformed; both, he said, were left behind by an exodus tragic in swelling dimensions and ominous in its significance for the future of the faith.

"Of course," he went on, turning to me, "you will blame the rabbis. I will not say that they are not to blame. But they are not the only causes, nor the deepest. Compare ourselves with Christianity; our orthodoxy has not the organization of Catholicism; our reform is without the emotions of Protestantism. With neither organization, nor feelings, what would you have? The age is secular and secularizing. The religious motive is crossed by a thousand others, intimate, forceful and promising immediate results. What does Judaism promise? Orthodoxy appeals largely to fear, Reform to vanity, and while you can base a considerable religion on fear, you can't keep anything durable on vanity, for vanity follows the fashions, and mirrors itself by the approval of others. The fact is, we are too intellectual and reasonable. We ignore the genuine bases of religious loyalty, and dam up the well-springs of religious allegiance. Relatively, all the religious sects have grown in numbers but ours."

"I doubt that," interposed Nathan, a broker with strong convictions about the mission of Israel. "But suppose it's true, what's the reason?"

"Well, wouldn't you laugh at the idea of a Jewish Salvation Army? Of a Jewish Billy Sunday? There—you're laughing now. Don't we all sneer at the *Chassidim?* Do we make any provision for the encouragement and utilization of that change of mood and outlook which comes to each of us at least once in his lifetime, that emotional readjustment which the Christians call 'conversion,' 'being born anew,' 'undergoing a change of heart'? We do not. Bar Mitzvah is at best an intellectual phenomenon, at worst an orgy of food and presents. Nothing momentous comes with it into the lives of our children, nothing momentous grows from it. Religiously, it is an occasion for the rabbi to exercise an indifferent fancy; secularly, well, you've been to Bar Mitzvah parties. If real emotion emerges, we stifle it. We pride ourselves on our reason. Only the other day I heard the mighty one from Bashan, I mean Bethel, declare that Judaism is too logical to say that three are one. That's—"

"Oh, nobody minds him," I interrupted, "he's not representative. Besides, he talks through his hat most of the time. I'll bet you a hundred to one for the National Fund that he doesn't know anything about the Trinity, and is merely juggling vocabulary, setting 'three' over against 'one.' "

"He's one of our spiritual leaders, acknowledged as such. And what he knows or doesn't know is irrelevant. It's that ungodly insistence on 'logic.' Modern Judaism is so logical, that it's logically committing suicide. It's not that we are incapable of emotion, of a loyalty that springs from the very fibre of our being; it's merely that, being diverted from the religious object and being denied religious sanction, it turns elsewhere. Of course, Judaism pays,—while Christianity renews its life upon this emotion and grows stronger, even in a secular age."

"Very well. What would you have us do?" the broker retorted with some heat, "organize a Salvation Army, employ Billy Sunday and exploit 'conversion'?"

"Trying it out might do no harm; of course, we should need our own forms," said Cohen.

"I don't believe it would take you very far." This remark came from Levitan. Levitan makes his living by professing chemistry in an eastern university; his life is Zionism. "I admit," he added, addressing us generally, "the correctness of Cohen's analysis, but it doesn't go deep enough. It's true that modern Judaism tends to stop up and dry up the wells of emotion from which it must suck its life as a religion, but it is not by this that it condemns itself to death. If the various Christianities had the same relation to the rest of life as Judaism, they, even with their complete exploitation of feeling, would share the same fate. The fact is the converse. Christianity is integral to the social life of the Christian communities; through its forms and organization it suffuses every phase of the secular interests, so that even the political mood of the country has its Christian tone. Not so with Judaism. When it's orthodox, when it's a life, it has to keep itself separate from the streams of the life about it. It can't assimilate them because it has no base for its assimilative function, it's a stomach without a body, and either what it receives must pour through unaltered, or derange the organ. When it's reformed, it's in a worse quandary; it has changed from a container into a content. It gives up more than it saves, it loses color, flavor, individuality; it becomes, so far as it is itself concerned, an indistinguishable part of the environment to which it adapts itself. To maintain its pretense at individuality, it has made the most of dialectical instead of real differences, like the three-one business or the mission business. Ninety per cent. of your rabbis don't take any stock in the mission. Do they, Cohen?"

Cohen smiled. "What are you driving at, Levitan? What's this to do with our failure to utilize the basis of religious loyalty?"

"This; that you make the mistake of supposing that religion is a thing in itself and an end in itself. Well, it's neither. Vanity is a good motive to appeal to, but in our age even vanity shrinks from resting its claims upon the supernatural. That way lies the imputation of madness, and vanity can't endure imputations. That's why the laity is unaffected by the profession's prating about the mission of Israel, and the profession as a whole is letting the dogma die through desuetude. Beyond the notion of 'mission,' what do you offer to command the allegiance of the young? Anything in ethics by which you can claim superiority over the ethics of other people? Not to the college-bred. They know too much history and have too many contacts with non-Jews. The very program of 'modern Judaism' implies the superiority of the non-Jewish ways of living and thinking; for it teaches the abandonment of what they know as intrinsically Jewish. They learn very soon that being a Jew is being at a disadvantage, and that is what you really offer them, without the compensating other-worldliness, and without the pledge of power and happiness that Christianity offers the convert. So even if you had Billy Sundays and conversions, they wouldn't have the same effect. Your religion is too isolated, too detached from corporate interests of a natural and organic society."

"And the conclusion is—Zionism, I suppose," said Cohen, sadly.

"Yes, in one way or another. Only Zionism can save Judaism because only Zionism can supply it with an organic structure through which it can exercise its function; under present circumstances modern Judaism is thinking with a paretic brain or digesting with a cancerous stomach."

"Aw, cut it. You don't know what you're talking about," Nathan burst out, apoplectically. "You need to hear Rabbi Hirsch in Chicago several times. He'd show you. He'd show you how modern Judaism stopped apostasy, and how it showed we were some good in the world with our mission an' all."

"I dare say he would. But would he show me loyalty to Judaism on the part of educated men—not social loyalty —there's lots of that, but religious feeling, the absence of which Cohen here has been deploring? Could he show me the young bearing the burden of being Jews with joy and courage?"

"Do you think Zionism could, either?" asked Cohen, quietly.

"Yes, many, many times; yes."

"Well, come down to cases," Nathan challenged.

"I will. Of course, you all know Simon, at least by name. You all know what he has done in the world of physical chemistry, and you have all wondered at his curious activity as a Zionist. Nathan here regards it as absurd—a man like Simon, with his powers and reputation; and Cohen, you know you did, Cohen—resented his being a free thinker. It was Simon who made a Zionist of me, and Simon comes by his own Zionism altogether independently of any Jew or Jewish connections. He was, you know, a pupil of mine."

"He was!"

"Yes—that was ten—twelve years ago. I was assisting Richardson at the time. Interested in my work, and didn't care to be bothered by anything else. Simon came to me in his junior year, by way of the regular routine of getting advice about his courses. A long, frail-looking lad he was, just bursting with plans and ideas. Rather opinionated, but with a high-pressure quality that excused it. Besides, he was very young. At the time he was as much concerned about 'humanity' and social justice as about chemistry. He took to me. We have since agreed that it was because of the innate racial sympathy; we were at ease with each other, guards down. Of course, I wasn't shouting from the housetops that I was a Jew—and Simon, he was shouting that he was an American, and all his opinions were ortho-doxly cosmopolitan and international—differences be-tween people were merely social and economic, and all that, and a man's a man for all that. You know the talk. After a while we got from problems of physical chemistry to the Jewish problem. We used to walk around Fresh Pond, talking, or go into town to Charley's or sit half the night in my chambers. One evening he called me up over the 'phone. Must see me, he said, or he'd burst. We scarcely got sight of each other in the yard when he shouted, 'I'm a Zionist.'

"We went to town for dinner. Simon was plainly under great emotional stress. His eyes were shining and his glance remote. He kept taking my hand and letting it go. Through dinner he was silent. We walked back, and he didn't say a word. But his mood was infectious. I could feel he was uplifted and happy. When we got to my rooms he wouldn't go in. We walked all night.

"After an hour's walking like that he opened up. We hadn't exchanged personal confidences ever before, but now he poured out his whole story.

"He came from rather distinguished Sephardic stock, but his people, being the only family of the sect in the little western town where he was born, were members of the very respectable Ashkenazic congregation. His father was a rigorous pietist and hoped to make a rabbi of him. They did not get on well, and through the intervention of his mother Simon was sent east to school, his father having exacted a promise that he would carry out his daily religious obligations to the letter, and that he would refrain from eating meat. At school Simon had to fight for his promise, and lived up to it religiously the first year. The second year he was laughed and argued out of keeping it. Partly his schoolmates were responsible, partly his science master, who had taken a fancy to him. But it would have come anyhow; physics and chemistry are not compatible with revelation. He spent five years at that school. There were one or two other Jews there, but they were what our philosopher here calls amateur Gentiles. Simon rather despised them, though he speedily acquired their attitude toward his people. His associates were exclusively Gentiles, he went to their homes and met their sisters and sweethearts, he lived their lives. His own people did not gain by the contrast. Between him and his father a growing coolness became a complete separation. After his second vacation at home he did not return. His scholarly excellence assured him his education, and the interest of his science-master got him tutoring enough to yield him more than a living. His science-master was a rather unusual man—more like a master in an English public school than an American pedagogue. He was the author of one or two travel books, and wrote a great deal in the weeklies on politics. He had a humanitarian passion that was almost Jewish. His hobby was 'Americanism.' America, the quintessence of humanity; America, democracy; America, social justice; America saving the world through freedom. I am not sure that the man's passion, which was literary and mystical, did not attract Simon much more than his adequate scientific good sense. For theology and religion he had no patience; he would argue hours at a time, with overwhelming recitation of data, that the institution was the enemy of mankind. Simon, himself raw from his experience with God's champions at home, identified himself unconsciously but completely with Tolman's point of view.

"He brought that point of view to college, and he bought his anti-Semitism to college. He didn't exchange a word with a Jew in the first two years, and he was particularly vindictive in denouncing his people for capitalism. In his classroom and campus activities he had it all his own way. You know his charm. It outweighed even his dogmatism and volubility. If anybody ever turned Americanism into a fetish, he did. He took it to the settlements, where he preached it to Italians—he wouldn't have anything to do with Jews—and he took it to keg parties, where he preached it to undergraduates. His Americanism it was that made a Zionist of him. He was constantly adding to his always heavy schedule courses in American history and American literature. It was one of the latter that undid him, that same year that we got acquainted.

"He used to tell me about that course. He had a way of raising into a philosophic issue whatever notion was flitting through his mind at the time, and of then dropping it. But he kept reverting to that course in almost every confab we had during the term. His 'Americanism' had, he discovered, unconsidered origins and roots. Its beginnings were nourished by a tradition that he despised, because belonging to it had hurt him. That he was alert to it, deep down in his heart, that he was living in the presence of it day and night, his resentments showed plainly. If he'd been really free of it, he'd have been indifferent to it. Its hold on him was measurable by his feeling toward it. At first he wouldn't endure the notion that Americanism owed anything to the Hebraic tradition; he used to spend long hours elaborating dialectic to prove it wasn't so. He kept going for the professor in the course, who was a friend as well as a teacher, just badgering him. Of course, he didn't keep his personal problem out of the question, so it ended with the professor's letting out on him. The professor knew his history, you see. He told him that he was really a coward and a sham, passing as something that he really wasn't. He told him that he was disgracing a great tradition. He told him the meaning of *noblesse oblige* for Jews. Simon was dumbfounded. He had had no idea that he might be cutting so poor a figure in the eyes of others. He had rather fancied himself in the rôle of cosmopolitan and so on, and here he found his cosmopolitanism demonstrated a mere provincialism of vanity. Of course, he was humbled. Further talks with the professor followed. He began to seek out Jews in the settlement and in his classes. He acquired a curiosity about Jewish history, particularly Jewish social history. He balked at religion, and couldn't even be persuaded to enter a synagogue in curiosity. He forced me to accompany him on a good many of his social expeditions. On one of these we struck a Zionist meeting. Simon rather sneered at the idea at first. He took it to his professor, who was familiar with it, and in talking it out with him Simon acquired that whole *anschauung* of civilization and the place of the Jews in it with which his name had been identified. Of course, he didn't know that; the process was long, and slow, and subconscious. When it broke through to consciousness that night it had all the force of a sudden revelation, and a conversion. But there was nothing sudden about it. I was conscious of my own processes all the time, so that I woke into Zionism as normally as I wake from sleep."

"But what," said Cohen, "what about Simon's Judaism?"

"I was coming to that. Simon's theology isn't any different from what it was, but since he has become a militant Jew, a Zionist, he has learned to regard the religion of the Jews as essential and organic a part of Jewish life as all the rest. I have heard him defending it on what I should have called obscurantist grounds. But that apart, he has developed a sympathy and appreciation of religion I should have regarded impossible in the boy I knew ten years ago. You'll find in his house, Cohen, something that I'll bet you can't find in the house of any 'modern' rabbi in the country."

"What?"

"A kosher table."

1916

VII

JUDAISM BY PROXY

In spite of the efforts and the clamour of the rabbis the Jews of this country are on the whole uninterested in Judaism. This is truer of the members of the reformed sects than of the adherents to orthodoxy, but it is true of both. Only women and old men attend the synagogues and participate in the activities of synagogal life. The young and alert content themselves with formal membership and occasional, sometimes very occasional, perfunctory attendance. In point of fact, Judaism is sharing the fate which first befell Christianity at the period of the Reformation. Protestant Christianity arose as a modernization of Catholicism; it developed in an attempt to make religious thought and religious organization square with the knowledge and the living interests of the changing times. This attempt has been continuous since the beginning of the sixteenth century, and the Protestant camp is in fact the camp of progress in science and social reform. But progress is a secular, not a religious ideal, for religion is eternalistic, so that the religious community, in order to keep a place in life, had to adopt its pace and assume its forms. It learned to take orders instead of continuing to give them and the more advanced Protestant sects have shifted their emphasis from the promulgation of creeds to the prosecution of social programs. Ignorant faith has given way to intelligent works—the change shifting from interest in a compulsory way of believing for the sake of getting happiness in heaven to interest in an organized way of doing for the sake of securing decency on earth.

In a word, the other-worldliness which distinguishes Christian doctrine and which is the essence of all religions of disillusion has been displaced by a rising social intelligence. There has emerged a reinterpretation of religion which identifies it with social consciousness, and latterly Mr. Mordecai M. Kaplan, in some admirable bits of special pleading in the *Menorah Journal,* has applied this reinterpretation to Judaism. Social consciousness and intelligence are, however, a secular and not a religious thing, and their operation in the field of religion is an evidence of the tremendous degree of secularization which the Protestant sects and even Judaism have undergone in the latter quarter of the last century.

Reform came to Judaism three centuries later than it came to Christianity. This is not due to any higher degree of preoccupation with religion on the part of the Jews, but to the fact that they were cut off from the streams of new thought and feeling which influenced the minds of the Christian communities. These began to infiltrate the ghetto toward the end of the eighteenth century, but the nineteenth had passed its noon before any genuine change got noticeably effected. Jewish Protestantism was both more radical and more destructive than Christian Protestantism. The reason is that the Christian religion is of a nature alien to and superimposed upon the national life and the genius of the Christian peoples. It had from the outset to undergo a process of assimilation and reconstruction that should fit it to those qualities. Judaism is not so. Judaism is an organic constituent of the life of the Jewish group, and if it is to survive it can do so only as one aspect of the total expression of the inwardness of the national genius of the Jewish people. Among the familiar religions of Europe, it is the *national* religion *par excellence*, and its place in the organic total of Jewish life is indisputable and important. This fact is for good reasons not so apparent with respect to the reformed sect, but consideration of the color and qualities of orthodoxy will make it clear. The daily life of the orthodox Jew is religiously regulated from the moment he arises in the morning to the moment he returns to his bed. All his enterprises, all his business, all his pleasures, in all their minutiae, are attached to divinity and sanctioned or condemned by divinity. His rabbi is not merely his "religious teacher," he is the judge of his community, the administrator of the traditional law of his people as that has been formulated in Talmud and Shulchan Aruch. His functions touch Jewish life at all points. In orthodoxy religion is life and life is religion. Orthodox laymen are often the peers of their rabbis in the knowledge and practice of Judaism, Judaism involving *all* their interests. Orthodoxy is, in a word, a way of living.

What the Jewish reformation did was to separate the communal from the religious life of the Jews. Religion, instead of requiring the definite organization of the daily life under the law of God, was made to require merely a declaration of belief. Judaists of the reformed sects may and do live as their Gentile neighbors may and do live. Their rabbi is not the administrator of the law; primarily he is their expounder of faith. He promulgates the dogmas of their religion for them, dispenses their charity, educates their children in their dogmas—and for the rest is irrelevant to their waking lives. The course and substance of those are assimilated, so far as Gentiles permit it, to the life of the Gentiles. Reformed Judaism, in a word, is, practically considered, a way of talking.

I have heard rabbis of the reformed sect, such as Mr.

Hirsch of Chicago, declare that reform alone could have saved numbers of Jews from apostasy. While it is an open question whether the numbers led by it to apostasy do not equal or exceed the number that are saved by it, the statement is undoubtedly correct. For the fact is that under the stress of a secular and secularizing age Judaism disintegrates much more rapidly than Christianity. This disintegration owes its rapidity to the peculiarly national character of the Jewish religion. This quality is the cause also of the strange anomaly into which the Judaistic reformation has fallen.

On the whole, reformed and orthodox Judaism can hardly be said to be any longer commensurable. However close they may lie doctrinally, they are practically as opposed as the poles. Orthodoxy is undoubtedly losing adherents to reform, as reform is losing them to Christian Science, agnosticism, and intelligence. The change, from one Judaistic sect to another, it must be remarked, does not, on the part of those who make it, indicate a change of opinion; it indicates a change in economic status and the existence of social ambition, reform being the sect of the rich, and orthodoxy of the poor. Orthodoxy, however, has power which is rooted in its social and organic character. If once the rich affect it, it can go on its own force, as the history of the surviving Sephardic communities shows. But reform has no inner resources.

Anybody who is familiar with the elementary principles which govern the play of passion we call interest will understand this. Interest is developed and preserved by action and the range and variety of our action is motivated by the fundamental instincts that are at work in the preservation and the enrichment of life. Doctrines which do not require a *specific kind of conduct* have consequently very little hold on the minds of those who hold them. They are interchangeable with other doctrines. They do not affect the course of life in any definite, recognizable way. The transition from reform to Christian Science demands only a change in the formula of belief, in the way of talking, not in the way of living. It is like changing from 2 x 2 equals 4 to 12–8 equals 4. The practical result is the same. But the transition from orthodoxy to reform involves a cataclysm which may reshape the convert to the very root of his being. It means, if really carried out, if carried out in the conduct of the daily life, surrender of personal habits, alteration of social obligations, of standards and methods of conduct, of thought, of all the complex activities that constitute the man's life. It means this because orthodoxy *is* a life. But such a surrender cannot possibly be made *in toto*. Consequently, you see men ostensibly adhering to the dogmas of the reformed sect who live the life of orthodox Judaists, and so profound are their habits, moreover, that it seems almost inevitable to them that their children should share them. Whatever their belief may be, their Judaism is not vicarious, because it is a personal participation in the communal activities sanctioned by religion for the whole race.

The case of the layman of the reformed sect who has been brought up under its teachings is quite different. His life is secular to the last degree. He takes his Judaism by proxy. His association with his fellow-members of sect and synagogue depends partly on the natural inertia of the human mind, which makes for the least action possible, partly on the social connections established in childhood, partly on the exclusiveness of the Gentile. Hence Jews of the Gilded Ghetto find it more comfortable on the whole to live with each other than to live with Gentiles whose habits and manners of life have become their accepted standards. The overt point of departure for their mode of association is the "temple," its culmination is a social club. For the rest, the actual responsibilities which a Judaist would have as a Judaist are delegated to the rabbis. Because his religion is not implied in the specific actions of his daily life, the Judaist of the reformed sect grows up profoundly ignorant of the history and the doctrine of his sect. He is familiar with the imputed glories of the Jewish monopoly of monotheism and with the doctrine of the mission. This stimulates his vanity and gives him a sense of cosmic importance. He is still a member of the chosen people, although the election implies for him no particular responsibilities, no knowledge, no action. His beatitude comes as a miracle from the Lord and he is content to let it go at that.

The effect on the rabbis by way of reaction, seems on the whole to be disastrous. They become the sole seats of authority and sources of information concerning Jews, Judaism and Jewish problems. To them is delegated all the responsibility for Jewishness which may pertain to the individual. In consequence, a generation of this sort of thing has developed a new orthodoxy—the orthodoxy of the reformed sect, and the spiritual relations between the rabbis of the sect and their flocks has become very like that between the Catholic priesthood and its flocks. The laymen of both reform Judaism and Roman Catholic Christianity are completely and essentially ignorant of the substance of their religions. The clerics of both groups lay down the law definitely and finally. So far as the laymen are concerned they exercise in matters religious a certain infallibility. With this difference, however. The individual cleric in the Catholic Church is a unit in an organization with a fixed body of doctrine to which he must defer. The cleric in the reform Judaistic sect is autonomous. His dogmatism is on the whole anarchic. One often

gets the impression of this or that rabbi as a little pope
with a tendency to modify practices, particularly, as suits
his convenience. Thus, there has grown up, in the not too
ancient tradition of the reformed Synagogue in America
the practice of "confirming" the young at *Shabuoth*. There
is, I dare say, no infallible authority for the practice. But
it *is* a form of communal action which has grown up naturally and spontaneously. It possesses the weight and
sanction that should pertain to any group custom. When
it failed, however, to suit the convenience of a prominent
Chicago rabbi the confirmation period was set at rather
an earlier time and the alteration acrimoniously defended
by challenging the authority of the custom.

On the other hand, in matters of essential thought, reformed doctrine has shown itself without power to develop, without the potency of growth. In reform far more
than in orthodoxy men seem to me to be subject to the
rule of dead minds. Doctrine, we must always remember,
does not arise *in vacuo*. Whether we attribute to it a
supernatural origin or not, it has a definite bearing on
social conditions, particularly on the evil in them, and is
created in order to mitigate or abolish the evil. The religions of *other*-worldliness arise at a time when this world
is very bad. A doctrine of the natural and inalienable
rights of men develops in politics when a doctrine of the
divine rights of kings works disastrous practical effects,
and so on.

Our social and religious theories and beliefs are to a
very small degree descriptions of the world as it is; mostly
they are postulations of the world as we want it to be.
Reformed Judaism is in itself a phase of the democracy
of protest and the social abstractionism and cosmopolitanism of that part of the nineteenth century which was trying
to turn dynastic and tyrannical government into consti-

tutional and free government. So, for example, the assertion that all men are created by nature equal is, taken
by itself, altogether false. But as an instrument, as a means
with which to equalize the unnatural inequalities against
which it was directed, it was true enough. It was true,
that is, in a social setting and for a purpose. It did not
describe a fact, it expressed a protest. Today this doctrine has undergone a great deal of modification. We say
now that the equality with which all men were created
is only equality of opportunity and not equality of nature.
The formula has been retained, but its meaning has
changed with the conditions and needs of the times. There
is not observable, however, in the doctrine of official Reformed Judaism any analogous change. The teachings of
the school at Cincinnati and its protagonists are actually
what they were when reform was first promulgated. It
ignores the tremendous social, economic and political
changes which the last century brought mankind. It ignores the changes in thought and feeling which Europe
has undergone and which have given a new and realistic
meaning to democracy, to liberty, to social justice. It is
a sort of spiritual infantilism, and the Reverend Mr. Schulman calls it "Modern Judaism."

But nothing could be more out of touch with *living*
modernity. For it is of the nineteenth century, and life
is of the twentieth. The reason seems to be that reform
is so detached from *Jewish* life, so little a matter of
community action, and consequently so little a matter
of community interest. Orthodoxy, at least in Europe, because it involves a whole complex of habits of living and
doing, is incapable of developing an infallible priesthood.
The rabbis are always confronted by learned laymen
who, without having any ecclesiastical authority have
tremendous influence on the opinion and doctrine of the

church in the course of living itself. Because orthodoxy is a *life* it possesses a dynamic principle which may carry it on and perhaps save it in the face of the widening circles of secularization. Reform, however, is a faith merely. It tends in the long run to be more and more an easy way out of Judaism. From Judaism by proxy to no Judaism at all, is only a matter of a generation or two.

I do not wish to be understood as putting the onus of the problem this condition presents upon reformed Judaism alone. Orthodoxy is undergoing an analogous fate. If I stress the condition of reform more it is because I regard reform as holding thus far the obvious economic and social leadership of the American Jewish communities and as having, consequently, all the responsibilities of leadership.

Orthodoxy is a life, but to lead it in an environment such as our century offers, requires a firmness of will and an intensity of vision which I regretfully fail to discern in the attitude of the Jews in different parts of the land who come annually under my eye. It is inevitable, and it is also just and proper, that the vision they begin with should be deepened and broadened by all the streams of thought and feeling that flow from the cultures of the nations. It is inevitable, and it is also just and proper, that they should realize that human life in any of its rich and varied forms and organizations, needs no supernatural sanction and no supernatural menace to keep it upright, just, and noble. When education abolishes both sanction and menace for them, they imagine, however, very naturally but also very disastrously, that the mode of living which these enforce is deprived of its significance and dignity. That is an error. All group life has its specific excellences, intrinsically justified, and the social customs which are the *effective* content of orthodoxy are not the less desirable and Jewish when we learn that they are human and relative. As mere customs and habits, however, they cannot resist the attrition worked by association with the Gentile neighbor. They need a community ideal to sustain them, and they need it in a world which is secular and is, fortunately for the hopes of mankind, growing more so. Because of this a reversion from reform to orthodoxy is impossible, even if it were desirable. The failure of young Mr. Magnes's spirited attempt to bring about such a reversion seems to me conclusive on this point, and I do not believe that any other man would have succeeded either. For while temperament plays a large rôle in leadership, social trend-and-bias itself determines temperament, and whatever the shortcomings attributed to Mr. Magnes as a leader, religious or otherwise, they would have made very little difference if the intellectual and social situation had been favorable. In merely its religious aspects, the future of the Jewish spirit in this country and anywhere in the western world strikes me as being very dark. Nor the future of Judaism merely; the future of all religions. On the whole supernaturalism cannot maintain itself against a practical intelligence which wrests her secrets from nature and makes the world more habitable by using them. Secularization comes on apace. Its progress is marked by the shift of the interest of the Christian sects from the other world to this; by their substituting the new interest in social justice for the old interest in salvation.

Judaism, if it is to survive, must accept and conquer the actual conditions of survival. These conditions lie in the relevance to the actual living interests of Jewry as those affect the daily life and personal habits of individuals in their relations with each other. They are the substance of what makes a community. But because the Jewish community is one among many in this country, these customs and habits cannot go on their own power. They need an animating ideal. In the twentieth century, with its growing realization of group individuality, its conception of democracy as the free interplay and co-operation of group-individuals as well as single persons, this ideal is inevitably the historic personality of the Jewish people, that social and spiritual complex of group qualities and customs which constitute nationality. That alone can supplement and strengthen, and if need be, replace, the failing supernaturalism which has until the beginning of the nineteenth century played so large a rôle in the integration of the Jewish community. Today in the modern, democratic world, the integrating force which articulates nationality is Zionism. Zionism alone can turn Judaism by proxy into Judaism by practice.

1916

VIII

JEWISH QUARRELS AND JEWISH UNITY

As the alignment of masses and classes, democracy and oligarchy grows more definite and distinct in the course of the controversy over the holding of a Jewish Congress, and the apparent chasm between different groups in Israel seems to widen with the days, my mind keeps reverting to the wise words of Judge Mayer Sulzberger, before the Intercollegiate Menorah Society. It was last December, at the annual dinner. Besides the Menorahites, Jews of all shades and patterns of opinion were present—Cyrus Adler, of the American Jewish Committee, rabbis orthodox and reformed, assimilationists who came out of curiosity, and, of course, Zionists. Addressing himself to all these, but particularly to the young men and women of the Menorah Association, Judge Sulzberger said: "I do not trouble myself much about definitions of Jews and Judaism. I do not think very highly of the learned talk I have heard about race and nationality and a variety of other things. . . . I do not think that any of you can now or ever will learn to define Jews and Judaism. . . . The Jews are a fact and that is all; that is old. They are a fact thousands of years old and they need no definition, and if they did your definitions would be good for nothing. Nor is it your definitions that you are anxious about. It is the definitions of the others that are troubling you. The others are not troubling about your nationalism, or your Zionism, or your conferences, or your congress, or your

78

democratic representation—not a bit of it. For them you are one, indivisible, inside and outside, a Jew. The great world outside does not bother about your misunderstandings."

This puts the situation admirably, and its implications are worth developing. I have a feeling that Judge Sulzberger spoke from his heart, off guard, and that some of the implications of the fact which his ripe widsom acknowledges might be unwelcome to him. I recall Dr. Cyrus Adler's suggesting to me that his Honor did not mean what he said. But that is neither here nor there. It is profoundly true that to the outer world a Jew is a Jew, a fact, one and indivisible. The situation is not, however, so simple. The fact, Jew, is not defined alone by the attitude of the Gentile. It is defined also by the character of the Jew, his historic character, his social character, his spiritual character. These make up the persistent fact, about which theories may come and theories may go, while it endures, I will not say, forever.

Nor is this the whole story. For facts bear a very dynamic relation to the theories. Theories are not born out of the ether, nor are they sport of a fertile and jocund nature. They do not arise without a demand and they do not persist unless they somehow satisfy this demand.

Now, the chief cause of the demand for theories is fact. Fact falls into two classes: first, that to which we are well adjusted, which is harmonious to our interests, and an occasion for prosperity and well-being; and second, that to which we are ill-adjusted, which is inharmonious with our interests and is an occasion for misery and unhappiness. A toothache is a fact also, and it is the kind of fact which a toothache is that gives rise to theories. There is no problem of the good in life; evil alone makes a problem and requires a theory to explain it. If we Jews are fruitful of many conflicting theories concerning the fact of our Jewish existence, these theories mean that we are not in harmony with ourselves, nor with each other, nor with the world; that we find being Jews a disability. The theories are intended to mitigate the disability, to explain it away.

Thus, protagonists of the clergy of the reformed sect have recently been thundering in the index that the Jewish people are merely a religious sect. Their theory concerning the nature of the people ignores the people's history, ideals, contemporary achievements, life and interests. It is the theory which a minority is trying to force on the majority. It is a theory which arose to mitigate the political and social disabilities of the Jews at the beginning of the 19th century. It sought to convert Jews into Germans or Frenchmen or Englishmen of the Mosaic persuasion. Orthodox Judaism does not even consider it. These lovers of the flesh-pots who urge it now, urge it out of fear that the political and social gains which a century of democratic endeavor has brought to Jews, quite independently of any modification of Jewish theology, may be endangered by the acknowledgment of a fact which neither the majority of the Jews nor any of the Gentiles have ever questioned.

Others, again, would-be anthropologists or cosmopolitans, invent a theory which denies all reality to the social fact called the Jewish people. One proves by manipulating statistics that there is no such thing as a Jewish race, and that consequently none of the effects of the existence of such a race ought to follow. Another proves that the differences between human groups are due purely to economic status and environment, and that consequently there are no Jews or Gentiles, only workingmen and capitalists. But the "Jewish problem" persists, none the less, and the "genosse" goes on living in his socialist ghetto, with Jews and among Jews, and the anthropologist makes his living within the Jewish group as a Jew, if not as a Judaist.

Within these "schools" of interpretation of the fact of Jewish nationality there are, moreover, the ordinary sub-divisions, geographical, economic or social. The Jew is hyphenated as rich and poor, orthodox and reformed, Russian and German and Polish and Austrian and what not. Such modifications of the substantive Jew further complicate the problem which the Jew is to himself and to his neighbor. Men forget that these modifications are put on and taken off as we put on and take off our clothes. They lose their sense of the enduring fact which makes these differences possible and relevant.

Their theorizing and hyphenating only serves to complicate the fact, so that many of us, misled by theories, go shipwreck on the fact. It holds us invincibly; we dodge around it, under and over it, we batter ourselves against it, we become amateur Gentiles and split our souls upon it. Zangwill has somewhere a striking verse:

Hear, O Israel, the Lord, our God is One
But Israel, his people is dual, and therefore undone!

The duality lies in the attempt to disintegrate the organic unity of Hebraism, to disintegrate the fact of the Jewish community or group with all its social and spiritual qualities, institutions, history and ideals into that particular special thing which some theory, representing a vested interest or standing for an unsatisfied wish, declares it to be. Religion, in particular, has suffered thereby. Jews are a social minority in an overwhelmingly larger social environment. Contacts are problems. The reformed sect, to solve the problems, began to make concessions to the environment. In its extreme form it lost all differentiae which distinguished Jewish religion from the religions of the neighboring peoples. Save that its communicants are Jews "by race," it might as well be a Christian sect. Their children pass on, to materialistic lives or other sects not Jewish. Under environmental pressure, reform deliquesces. The orthodox sects, to solve the problems, emphasized ritualistic rigor. They stiffened to resist environmental pressure. Stiffening, they petrified. Neither do their young remain in the synagogue.

But do these youth, the flower and the promise of the people, cease thereby to be Jews? Yes, if the sectarian theorists are assented to. In fact, no. They may cease to be Judaists, they do not cease to be Jews. A Jew grows. A Judaist is made. We do not suck in Judaism with the mother's milk. We learn it in the Talmud Torah and the Sunday school, and if we don't like it as we learn it, we start a reformed sect or abandon it altogether. The fact of being a Jew is the fact of being a member of a natural social group, of a brotherhood of unforgotten ancient origin, who, because of their acknowledged social continuity, because of their likemindedness, develop a common life of social organization, religion, art, science and philosophy; develop, in a word, a common culture. Such a group is not a sect, not a party, not a state. But it is the common ground for sects, parties, and states. Those others are artificial. You can destroy them without destroying the individuals that compose them. For example, today you are a Judaist of the reformed sect; tomorrow you are a Christian Scientist; today you believe in the "Conference"; tomorrow you are intelligent and believe in the "Congress"; today you are a Pennsylvanian; tomorrow you are a citizen of California; or, like Mr. Astor, the rich man, or Mr. Henry James, the literary man, today you are a citizen of the United States, tomorrow you are a citizen of Great Britain. You cease to be these things without ceasing to be. But you cannot cease to be a Jew without ceasing to be. The Jewish group is the natural group to which you belong. A natural group is one which cannot be destroyed without destroying the individuals that belong to it.

The fact of being a Jew is the fact of belonging to such a group. As Judge Sulzberger, drawing his example from the life of Theodore Herzl, has beautifully shown—you may repress it, you may conceal it, you may make it the negation of your life and ideals. If you do, it becomes your Nemesis. Sooner or later it will manifest itself in the foreground of your life, even as it works unceasingly in its background. For it is the root of your nature and character, the dynamic of your activities, the basis of your failure or success. And you succeed or fail in the degree that it gets free play. In you, it is your "heredity." About you, it is your brothers and sisters, your cousins, your community—those who, being of the same *breed*, the same family, have the same mind as you. This group mind is the culture of your group—its history, its forms of social organization, its art, its religion, its every expression in thought and things, of its inward spirit. This group mind, in the Jew, is Hebraism.

Cultures, you will see, possess a nature as organic as the physical form of life. Just as in temperament and in power you cannot separate yourself from your ancestors, from your heredity; or in health, you cannot separate the condition of one of your organs—of your lungs or heart or brain or liver—from the rest, so you cannot separate any social institution from the natural community-complex of which it is a part. To do so is to kill it, and in so far as the rabbis have detached Judaism from the total complex of *Jewish* life, they have condemned it to death. Life is organic; you cannot breed a feather without breeding a whole chicken, nor a living heart without a whole living body. You cannot convert the Jewish community into a mere sect without destroying Judaism. Judaism as Judaism can flourish only in the organic wholesomeness of Jewish communal life, with its checks and counterchecks, its conflicts, adjustments, and balancings of opposed parts. Only by reintegrating Judaism into the wholeness can it be saved.

This is why I, as a Zionist, find something unthinking in what each theorist tries to do to the fact of Jewishness. For each lays stress on some particular part or aspect of the whole; each seeks, in fact, to substitute this part for the whole. In religion orthodoxy is more organic than reform, however, for orthodoxy is a *way of living,* while reform is only a way of talking.

As a Zionist I am concerned about the *wholeness* of the Jewish spirit, that wholeness in which each tendency, each party, exercises a particular organic function, as the organs of the body do in the body. I welcome them all, I acknowledge them all; orthodox and radical, sectarian and nationalist. However much they may deny it, their addressing each other, their quarreling and debating with each other, diseased as this often is, is a complete acknowledgment of how dependent upon each other they are. If the Jews were really a sect, the sectarians would be at no such pains to prove it; if the Jews were as integrally a nation as they are a nationality, the nationalists would not be so ardent. In point of fact, all these parties are members of one another, dependent upon one another for their existence. Together, not in isolation, they constitute that social fact, the Jewish people.

The same thing is true with respect to the issue of the Jewish Congress, the issue which has aroused so much passion and so much bitterness. The conflict between those who believe in the Congress and those who do not is a conflict between two parties in the Jewish nationality. Logically, those who think Jewry is not a nationality should not participate in the conflict. But the conflict is not a matter of logic. It is a matter of life, and its very existence testifies to the unity of the Jewish people. The parties to the conflict are older than we are; they are older than our fathers and our grandfathers. They have their roots in those parties whom the prophets represented and those whom the prophets attacked. Only the crisis which the European war created brought this conflict to an acute issue now, and not ten years later. It is a conflict involved in the very structure of American society, in the inward character of the general reorganization of the Jewish community that the Americanization of the great Jewish masses is bringing about. If the Jewish people in America did not feel themselves to be one, as at least the members of a family are one, the issue could never have been joined. If the parties had never a common purpose, they would never quarrel about separate means for carrying out their purpose.

Often, however, means become an idol, a fetish. The end for which they exist is forgotten. A party which got into power by virtue of service may seek to stay in power for the sake of power. A class, privileged by accident and opportunity, may seek to keep its privilege at any cost, adopting the policy of "rule or ruin." Such parties and classes forget that leadership, in a land like ours and in times like ours, is representative, that it can be maintained only by expressing the will of the people, not by opposing it. They act blindly, without counting the conditions and costs of action. They will denounce a possible speech not yet made, by some poor anonymous devil of a radical for the effect it might have on the Russian government's

attitude toward the Jew, and publicly refuse to participate in a Russian loan because of the Russian government's treatment of the Jews. They will commit any number of ironical contradictions and absurdities rather than
acknowledge and accept the conditions of leadership as
those are set by the social situation in our American
democracy.

To such classes and their analogues in religious organizations, fraternal orders and so on, Judge Sulzberger's
words may be directed with apt timeliness. Their significance cannot be overestimated. The Jew is a fact. The
very quarrels within Jewry are only a confirmation of this
fact. The Gentile ignores those quarrels; all Jews look
alike to him. His attitude, his good-will or malice, defines
the status of *every* Jew, not of this or that particular class
or group. If the unity which the Jew has in the eyes of the
non-Jew is not confirmed by a greater unanimity on the
part of the Jew, what shall be the fate of the crucified
millions in the Russian pale? Or, for that matter, of the
enfranchised Jew of the Western world? And what are
the conditions of unanimity in the free society of America?

1916

IX

THE PLACE OF JUDAISM IN THE JEWISH PROBLEM

In the history of civilization, religion is among the first principles of conscious difference between different groups. The reason is that in historic times the human group which has its way to make in this troubled world imagines it to be composed of material seen and psychological unseen beings, of bodies and of souls. All primitive peoples think that behind the world that they behold, behind each tree, each mountain, each river, each ocean, or inside of these things, there is an invisible soul. This soul they take to be exactly like the human soul, and if they want something from the forest or the river, they ask for it in exactly the same way that they ask from their neighbors. When you want something from your neighbor, you really pray to him for it. You say, "Won't you please give me this or that?" with the tacit understanding that you will endeavor to return the favor in some way.

But when you pray to the gods you usually reverse this procedure, for you give the gods something first. You make a sacrifice in return for which you expect to get the results you ask for. So, when there is a birth, when puberty comes, when marriage is celebrated or death is mourned, when the ground is to be tilled, or a hunt or a battle to be undertaken, or a disease cured—in each one of these crises of life that have to do with the increase of the breed, with the food supply, with defence against the human or sub-human enemy, with shelter from climate— primitive mankind and modern both invoke the life in nature, because they look upon the life in nature as being like human life. Now when they think of nature as Ba-al, for example, and when they think of nature as Yahweh, or as Jupiter, or as Zeus, they are really defining nature in terms which vary with race and place.

And so also does the way in which they get at nature in order to specify their wishes. This way is the religious ritual, and the religious ritual is a certain organization of methods of thinking and doing and feeling, which becomes a form of expressed distinction between peoples. Primitive peoples differ from one another far more in their religions than in anything else. Every phase of their social order, what they think and do, their fighting, their loving, their digging of the soil, their hunting—everything—is controlled by this suppositious relation to the unseen powers. Their life is an enterprise which goes on as the dramatic triangle of man and God and nature. The primitive man never approaches nature directly. He approaches nature through God. The devices by which he uses divinity for this purpose, his behavior toward it, are the substance of his social organization and of the order and development of life; are his customs, his system of law and living. Whatever he does involves the unseen powers with which religion is supposed to concern itself. For him, therefore, life is religion and religion is life. In it, the cultural and civil differences between peoples are first manifest, and by it the distinctions between groups are first fixed and introduced. Men get classified according to the gods they worship, those being the obvious differentiae of community life. Nor, at first, are men much aware of any other distinction between one group and another, although such other distinctions do exist. The Jews were distinguished from the Canaanites basically because the Jews worshipped Yahweh and the Canaanites worshipped various Baals. The other distinctions—those of origin, mode of life, etc.,—were regarded as derivative from the gods and were not often in the minds of the worshippers. The gods implied everything and everything implied the gods. Thus, when history was young religion was the basic totality of civilization.

Experience and necessity, however, led to a division of labor. Little by little, men learn that the religious way of handling nature is not conducive to success. A man, for example, wants to cross a river. He assumes that the river is animated by a god, and before he steps into his canoe, he gets a bowl of milk and pours it into the river in order to propitiate its spirit. Then he enters his canoe and trusts to luck. Perhaps he reaches his destination without trouble. But the probability is that he falls into a great deal of trouble, and, if he does, then his obvious deduction is that his sacrifice has failed to please the god. Being on the river, he does the best he can, without the god's help, because he must. He pays attention to the current and to the other properties of the river which condition its navigation. Finally, he gets across without god's help. Then he depends not on his religious hypothesis but his scientific knowledge of the river. He has replaced religion with science. Science handles nature by direct control; religion handles it through a god. Little by little improvement in technical methods based upon increase in the positive knowledge of nature narrows the field of religion. A division of labor rises, and religion instead of being a way of all life becomes less than all life. It becomes only a part of life, having its own special and particular purpose.

The god of a nationality does not, however, thereby cease to be the principal distinction between one nationality and another. In antiquity nationality and religion are coincident. In the ancient Hebrew religion, for example, the god has only what is called ethnic sovereignty. This means that his power is co-extensive only with the territory his worshippers dominate. Thus Yahweh, as the god who lives on Sinai, cannot leave his holy mountain. When his people fare forth he goes not himself but sends his messengers with them. Only much later does he become a god of Canaan, and still later a god of the Universe. Because of the age-old co-ordination of a god with a tribe, a place and a habitation, ancient religion, in spite of the progressive rise of other social institutions through the division of labor, remains an expression of nationality. Each important god is the patron god of a nation. So Pallas Athene was the patron goddess of the Athenians, and her worship was more important to the Athenians than the worship of the other gods. She represented the spirit and content of their life and distinguished them from the other peoples. In a similar way, Yahweh represented the life of the Jews; Bel, Marduk, Isis, gods of Assyria, Babylonia and Egypt, were symbols of the spirit of the nationality of the princes and peoples to whom they pertained.

II

In the course of time and in very varying degrees, religion became universalized. The reason for this is not inherent in religion itself. The universalization was the effect of political changes in the Mediterranean civilization. This civilization resides, roughly, in a series of small nationalities, each one of which owns a particular god. Then one king after another, first Egyptian, then Assyrian, then Babylonian, then Persian, then Greek, then Roman, establishes a great empire, and the god of the

conqueror is declared to be victorious over the gods of
the conquered, a mightier god to whom the other gods
bow down.

In the Roman Empire, however, the political and social
interests of imperial government demanded much more
than this external subservience. It demanded the unifica-
tion of religion because the god was a symbol of the whole
state. The Roman Emperor required to be worshipped as
a god. And the connection between divinity and the ruling
power is everywhere permanent. Rulers either *are* divine
or divinely appointed. Alexander and his Greek successors, the emperors of Rome, all claimed at least divine
ancestry and honors. The kings of Judah were supposed
to be kings by divine appointment. In modern history this
survives as the "divine right of kings," and is defended
by the adherents of the Japanese or the German emperor.
The more extensive and powerful the rule, the more universal its divinity. So the unity of god and the omnipo-
tence of god is a function of the development of empire
in the ancient world, particularly of the development of
the Roman Empire.

Nevertheless, the Roman government was on the whole
very tolerant of the religions of its subject peoples and
regarded them as national and local subordinates to the
divinity of Empire. It built for every god of a subject
people a temple in Rome, hoping in that way to generate
in the different subject peoples the feeling of a certain
solidarity with each other, and of the hopelessness of opposition, since their very holies were in Rome and were
there maintained by the force and generosity of the ruling
political and military powers.

Now the post-Augustan Roman was not particularly
interested in religion as such. For a time, the ruling classes
were on the whole rather philosophically minded, and their

religions were more like philosophical systems, such as Stoicism and Epicureanism. The Jews, on the other hand, were as intensely interested in religion as ever, and having begun with certain beliefs regarding promises from Yahweh, they had great hopes of their own power and imperial domination over the whole world. These hopes, they found, experience was constantly frustrating. Instead of being rulers of the world, they were victims of successive conquerors. Experience consequently put forth a pregnant alternative: Either Yahweh was a weaker god than the gods of their conquerors, or the conquerors and their gods were the instruments and tools of Yahweh, whose purposes were to be realized in a cosmic instead of in a tribal way. They chose the latter alternative. In prophecies like Isaiah's, Yahweh becomes conceived of a single power ruling over the whole universe. Not only is he lord and ruler of Israel, but lord and ruler of all nations; they are the instruments in the realization of his providential designs. This way of thinking about god was taken over by Christianity. Under the give and take between Christianity and the other religions of the Roman Empire, the old Jewish jealousy for Yahweh was universalized to coincide with the newly-defined universality of the Hellenized old Jewish god and there began the tremendous religious intolerance of which the Jews became the first and remain the oldest victims.

The unity of the Roman Empire that had been symbolized by the divinity of a single man was a unity of many parts. In it each national god had received on the whole the same consideration as any other. But under the Christian rule this ended. There existed, the Christian theologians held, only one god and he was a monopolist. He would not tolerate the worship of any other imaginary divinity. He was a jealous god, and his glory and man's salvation required the destruction of those people who did not agree with his own worshippers. The Christian régime, therefore, from the council of Nice to the 19th century, was largely the régime of persecution and compulsory conformity in religion. During the Middle Ages Europe was single and unified in matters of dogma. But at great cost in human life and human happiness. And the unity was illusory. In point of fact, religion was not at all the same all over Europe any more than the races of men were the same. In point of fact, the Catholics of England and the Catholics of France, of Italy and of Germany were of different Catholicities, and they differed according to the nationality of the people who professed this general Christian religion. Under God, His Son and His Son's Mother, the national gods ruled as patron saints—St. George of England, St. Denis of France, and so on. Indeed, the national differences were so pronounced that the unity of Catholicism could be maintained only by the Inquisition and by the sword.

The Reformation finally broke Catholicism's enforced unity completely up, and the national alignment of Christian religions became, roughly speaking, once more the order of the day. The Latin peoples, who were accustomed to centralized organization and imperial rule, remained Catholic. France, Spain—particularly Spain—Italy, Southern Germany (which is of much the same ethnic culture as the French and Italians)—these are all Catholic. One people which is not Latin—the Polish people—is Catholic, not because it is natural for them to be so, but because it is a device for keeping them distinct from the hated Russians, who are Greek Catholics; the Poles use their Catholicism as an engine of nationality. All the northern peoples have divided into sects according to nationality. England has an Established Church which is quite different from the Lutheran organization of Germany, and this again is different from the Calvinism of Geneva and Holland, and that again is different from the religion of the Scandinavian countries. European Christianity is not one but many, each defined as much by its national characteristics as by any other, and each expressive of national distinctions. Even in the cases where the state is one, as, for example, the German Empire is one state, diversity in nationality involves diversity in religion. Bavaria is Catholic and Northern Germany is Protestant. Religious boundaries really designate differences in nationalities as political boundaries do not. Great Britain is another example. There are four religions which correspond to the four different nationalities. There is the Established Church of England, there is the religion of Calvin or the Presbyterian religion of the Scotch, and there is the Roman Catholicism of the Irish, and the Methodism of the Welsh. And these mark off much more sharply than the political boundaries the national distinctions between the people of Britain. Roman Catholic Ireland is a separate and distinct part of Great Britain. Presbyterian Scotland is a separate and distinct part, and so on.

III

There is only one people whose religious and political boundaries are not even relatively coincident, one people only which has religious boundaries but no political boundaries. This is the Jewish people. But even for them it is not so very true that there is not this coincidence, if you consider the Jewish population of Eastern Europe as that population which was politically designated by the charter granted to it by Casimir I. Then you will find that in the

Pale, or that part of the Polish kingdom to which the Jewish people were kept, they have a definite geographical and political boundary. You will find also, that if the charter of Casimir I had been maintained in force in later times, there would have been a coincidence of religious and political boundaries for the majority of the Jewish people. The destruction of the Polish kingdom carried with it the destruction of this coincidence. The resultant status of Jews in the Empire of the Russians, the retention of old and the oddities of new mediaeval political disabilities, all these made impossible the coincidence of political and religious boundaries. Consequently the religion of the Jewish people was distinguished from the religions of the other peoples, was thrown into the foreground, so that by it and not by their institutional organization were they designated and named. The position of the Jewish people in Christian theology made this event more or less inevitable. But there was nothing in Jewish life to make it inevitable.

That is why the tradition has developed—a tradition which the reform synagogue has cherished—that the Jews are a "religious people." It is a tradition resting in the historical accident that they are the only people whose religious and political boundaries are not conspicuously coincident.

In spite of this accident, however, religion remains national for the Jews, in a way in which it is not national for the rest of the world. The reason is this: Jewish social organization, through another historical accident, which is regarded as unfortunate by the rabbis of the reformed synagogue and by most candid historians must be regarded as an arrest of development, has retained its primitive integral religious sanction. The Jew's ways of living are attributed to a commandment from on high, and the social and civil and economic law of the Jew is identical with the religious law of the Jew.

This is not true for any other people. Take, for example, the people of the United States. In this country religion is not the sanction for the whole of life. Religion is only a part of life and a part made up of lesser parts, for there are many religions in America. To be an American citizen means not exclusively to be Christian or Judaist or Mohammedan or Christian Scientist. It means also to be a voter, a Republican or a Democrat, a carpenter, a soldier, a lover of books or of music, to be all of the other things that the life of the state permits or involves. In no modern state is religion co-extensive with life. If it were, religious freedom could not exist there. In the quite modern world, religion is only a part of life and a very small part of it; it differs with different people according to their culture. For the mass of Jews, however, religion has remained on the whole co-extensive with life. Not completely co-extensive with life, because Jewish life today, even where there are great masses of Jews, as in New York City or in the late Russian Pale, is much more extensive than Jewish religion. But still the fundamentals of life are established on a religious basis.

It is for this reason, that the difference between orthodox Judaism and reformed Judaism is no mere difference of creeds. The creeds of both of these, except with reference to the return to Palestine, are, broadly speaking, the same. The difference lies in the constitution of reformed and orthodox society. The reformed Jew lives like a Gentile; his religion is a way of thinking or believing; but it makes no material difference in his habits of living. The orthodox Jew, however, has a polity and an organized life all under religious prescription. By his religion the orthodox Jew is much closer to the ancient Jew's organization of life. He has retained the characteristics of antiquity. Note, please: The chief institution of orthodoxy is the synagogue. Next to the synagogue is the school system, which ranges from the Talmud Torah, through the Beth Hamidrash and the Yeshibah—an elaborate *gradus* which carries one from the elements of Hebrew learning through the whole labyrinthine system of Jewish law and Jewish thought. Now, these institutions can go on without involving any of the other implements of social organization, still Jews have to live and to die in accord with prescribed rules. The organization of the economic structure, which involves life's fundamentals, is prescribed in religious terms. Thus the institutions next in order of importance are the slaughter house, the bakery and the dairy. For the Jewish community must prepare its food ritually according to established law, and the preparation must have been sanctioned by the rabbi. Sanitary provisions about food are further supplemented by certain sanitary provisions about the person. Every properly organized Jewish community must have its public bath, or *mikwah*, and bathing must take place according to rule. And finally every community must have its Jewish burial ground.

Now the reformed synagogue retains the meeting house, calling it "temple" and the burial ground, but none of the other institutions. Yet these other institutions compose the basic units in the organization of Jewish life, and every one of these units is established according to the law of God, interpreted by a long and ancient line of rabbis. Furthermore, this life, which is called in this country congregational life but which is properly community life, is carried on primarily and fundamentally under Jewish law. The rabbi is not the "religious leader" merely, as is the reform rabbi. He is not merely the person who presides at the synagogue, looks after the Sunday school, and marries and buries his congregation. The rabbi of orthodoxy does all these things, of course, but his most important function is to be the civil judge of the community. His powers and duties are civil and social very much more than they are ritual. He is, if I may say so, the "squire" of his community. He is the administrator of the law, and this law is incorporated in a code book which is familiar to most people as the *Shulchan Aruch*. Everything comes under the rabbi's oversight—the right preparation of food, marriage and divorce, trade and other agreements, and so on. Every Jewish community has its Beth Din, where disputes are brought for decision. The rabbi is technically described as "Hattarat Horaah." He is the judge: he is the teacher and the administrator of civil law, that law being re-enforced by the over-belief of its religious origin.

Now, if the Jews had had, together with this communal autonomy, complete political autonomy; if they had been "sovereign" in their dealings with other peoples, there would not have been any difference of status between the Jewish people and any other people in Europe. But although this inner organization of the orthodox community remains complete and full and defines the Jewish social personality in apparently a Judaistic way, the definition is in point of fact national, because it involves the basic institutions of the Jews' common life. The disabilities under which they lived caused this form of organization to operate to their disadvantage in their relations with non-Jews. It prevented them in many ways from establishing contacts with their Gentile neighbors. A Jew could not dine at the house of a Gentile. He could not enter into intimate friendships. The sharing of commensal and other pleasures which is a minimal basis for developing community life were inhibited by the dietary and other prescriptions. Consequently, there existed always a potential conflict between the civil status of the Jewish people and their religious organization. The events of the French Revolution made this conflict actual. In it consists the religious aspect or phase of the Jewish problem. Jews have attempted to solve it in a variety of ways.

IV

The solutions, to my mind, only complicate the problem. All solutions turn of course, first of all, on the secularization of the Jewish community. When the aborigine who tried to take a trip down the river stopped praying and sacrificing to the spirit of the river and acquired knowledge of the character of the river currents, this knowledge, and the attitude toward the river which it creates, have become secular. Secularism, it will be seen, consists in finding natural to replace supernatural interpretations of the relationships and attitudes of men towards things and events. Life becomes secularized as the gods becomes less and less practically important to the detailed business of living. That life is completely secularized which has no place for the supernatural in its ordering. Few lives attain this status. Most of us live secularly to the point of trouble, to the point where knowledge quite fails us. Then we turn to God. When there is nothing else to say or to do, the spirit returns to the infantile and elemental for safety; the pathetic fallacy prevails. The hope in our hearts recreates and invokes a spirit kinder to us than the nature it animates.

To return to the Jews. They were, and the majority of them in Eastern Europe still are, a distinct and peculiar people in that their life, a national life which to a large degree has been attributed to its religious sanction, has been continuous and unbroken practically until the beginning of the 19th century. The Jews remained for over two thousand years a "religious" nationality—i. e. a nationality retaining also the primitive characteristics of nationality. These characteristics are a survival, partly because the Jews desired the survival, largely because of the attitude of the Christian world. The Jews, like the other peoples of Europe, suffered the limitations of the early Christian theory and method of life. These postponed science, postponed democracy, rendered dangerous, if not impossible, an intelligent approach to life's problems. The implications of the theology on which they rested was such as to set the Jews in Europe beyond the pale of the law and to make them the legitimate prey of anybody who wanted to do them harm. Much of this attitude toward the Jew remains in Eastern Europe to this day, and it recurs cyclically in the West at every social crisis.

With the French revolution, a new attitude developed among the Jews. The revolution brought democracy to Europe. Napoleon did not merely override the whole European continent from Spain to Russia. The victorious French armies brought with them not merely French force. They brought also the ideas of the French revolution, ideas that impregnated every one of the European states, even Spain, and awoke Russia. The new attitude it generated among the Jewish masses reinforced the movement that had begun a generation before among the Jewish classes. The attitude might be described as secularistic and the process of secularization of Jewry is the process of its modernization.

This process brings the Jewish mind into contact with the *living* streams of thought in the European world, the science, the art, the philosophy that had come to be since the Renaissance. Until the last quarter of the 18th century, the Jewish people had been very largely cut off from intellectual contact, from any sort of contact, with the surrounding world. They had been absorbed in the development of interpretations of the Talmudic law. Their inward history had been chiefly religio-legalistic history tempered by a mysticism of which the successive false Messiahs were the expression. But in the 18th century, the new Renaissance mode of thinking had matured and become part of the mind of Europe itself. Christianity had, to a large degree, given way before the development of positive science, at least among the intellectual classes. Jews began to be looked upon as essentially human beings, instead of as the outlaws accursed of God. Various emperors and various rulers in Europe began to play with plans for the liberation of the Jews. For example, Joseph II of Austria issued his famous edict which tried to establish schools for the Jews, tried to grant Jews civil rights, and which political circumstances afterwards caused him to revoke. In Prussia, Frederick II, who had enjoyed the influence of Voltaire, emulated his Austrian competitor. He was helped by the great German Jew, who had come into touch with the best German minds of the period—with Lessing and with Goethe— Moses Mendelssohn. Mendelssohn was in many ways the bridge between the secularism and whatever else was new in the spiritual life of the European world, and this complicated pagan-mediaeval religious national Jewish culture which had been cut off from the world. Mendelssohn became a Germanizer and the Germanism and the Germanization of the Jewish mind began with his German translation of the Bible. He was also a Hebraist animated by an interest in literature for its own sake, instead of for God's sake, and a philosopher interested also in philos-

ophy for its own sake. The infection of his example spread
swiftly among the thinking classes of Jews in Germany
and the Pale where the Jewish nationality resided.

Now, as the culture of Europe slowly infiltrated the
great Jewish community, a conflict arose within that part
of it which was orthodox. The rabbis, of course, were at
first tremendously opposed to the introduction of anything
secular or foreign into the "spiritual life" of their charges.
Particularly were the Hassidic rabbis so, they being
magicians and mystics, who had substituted emotion for
learning as the foundation of the religious life, and had
added fortune-telling to ritual. The new material, none the
less, slowly spread until it had become diffused throughout
the whole Jewish community. The community's attitude
toward it is to be observed in several effects. Secularism,
for one thing, modifies the character of Jewish nationality.
It changes that from an antiquated religious nationality
to something which would, other things being equal, either
cease to be nationality, quickly losing its identity through
intermarriage and other forms of assimilation, or to something which would become more flexible, more resilient
and stronger by virtue of the fresh spiritual suste-
nance to be drawn from contact with other nationalities.

On the exclusively religious side, however, Jewish life
was bound to become, whatever the event, either deliques-
cent or rigid. In western Europe and in America the latter
state accrues generally to orthodoxy. The greater the pressure of the outer world upon it, the more ossified the orthodox organization of life becomes, and the more brittle.
The young do not remain in the orthodox synagogue.
They break their connection with it, suddenly, and the
field of orthodoxy grows narrower and narrower. It is
unable to heal the breaks, is without recuperative power—

and in countries like France or Italy, where there is no immigration to sustain it, dies of decreptitude.

V

Such is one extreme. In the other extreme the religious institution is adjusted to welcome as widely as possible and to undergo as fully as possible the demulscent influence of the external world. That is the method of reform, and in consequence of that method the reformed community little by little disappears. It also is dependent on immigration. In the United States, for example, very few of the children of the earliest generation of the reformed community are now any longer in the synagogue. Some of them are Christian Scientists; some of them have become agnostics; large numbers of them have "assimilated," have dropped, so far as they could, their connection with the Jewish community. Reform deliquesces and flows away instead of drying out. At that, the influence of reform on orthodoxy has on the whole been liberalizing. The orthodox rigidity has gained some flexibility through the competition of reform. But the one really salutary change in Jewish life effected by reform has been not the "religious" alteration of the ritual and prayer book, but the social change consisting in the liberation of the Jewish woman.

On the whole, the disinterested historian is not likely to have a very high opinion of reform as a genuine liberalization of Judaism. When, however, he sums up its historical influence, the greatest praise that he can offer it—and there can be none greater—is that of its effect on the status of the Jewish woman. In orthodoxy, the Jewish woman used to be a secondary person, having no rights before God, or even before man. Her status in this world

and in the next was not an enviable one. The most she
could aspire to, as a pathetic story of Perez tells us, was
to be a footstool to her husband in heaven. Her husband,
if she was fortunate, led a life of sacred scholarship and
left the responsibility of the maintenance of his household
and himself with the woman. She was in many instances
its sole support. She not only bore the children, she earned
their bread and the bread of their Talmud-studying father. The effect of this phenomenon has been to develop
a certain independence and power in the women of Israel.
When the liberation in the Jewish community as such
came, chiefly through the influence of reform, giving her
before God nearly the same status as the male, the woman
outdistanced the Jewish man tremendously in the approach to the problems of modern life. I am frank to say
that if Jewish girls seem to strike a higher level of spirituality and power than Jewish men, it is because in the organization of the Jewish community in the eighteenth and
nineteenth centuries the weaker sex were burdened with
this practical responsibility. The woman kept her husband
and his children in food and clothing and shelter on earth
that he might lay up treasure in heaven, and aspired to
no better reward than to be his celestial footstool there.
I say again, even though reform has as yet failed to admit women to membership in the vestry, the great achievement of reform has been the liberation of woman.

Orthodoxy's program *in extremis* was a program of
medievalism and was destined to failure. Its history in
the United States and in every other country shows this.
You cannot, in a world of railroads and telegraphs and
printing machines, cut off any group from contact with the
rest of the world. You cannot any longer make a hermit of
the Jewish people or of any European people. The only

way to do that would be to take this people off to the North Pole, or wherever the influence of the civilized world cannot reach. All religions have given way to the pressure of industry, science and democracy, of the new life and the new learning. Judaism, no less compelled than the other religions to contact with these things, had either to give way entirely and dissolve in modernism, or to find a *modus vivendi* whereby modernity could be assimilated properly and turned into the substance of the new Jewish spirit—what might be called the Jewish spirt of modern times.

If the Jews themselves had been the only factors in the situation, the solution would have been simple enough. But they were not. The Gentile world had to be counted. There was, for instance, a complication in the peculiar economic status of the Jewish people. They had been outlawed from the soil, practically from the beginning of history; they had been cut off from developing, in the community itself, any of the more fundamental economic activities. They had not been permitted to be day laborers and farmers. They constituted in relation to the rest of the population an ambiguous estate, a class of middlemen, traders, artisans, manufacturers, factors, money-lenders. Such wealth as they possessed was personal property, never real property. They were nomads. They had, on the whole, international connections. Their economic relationship to their non-Jewish countrymen was hence always a problematical one, and when they came out in the wide world, as they did under the influence of reform, they found themselves strongly confronted by a new kind of anti-Semitism, which turned on a description of their economic status. They were called blood-suckers, usurers, money-lenders; and civil rights, even when granted, were withheld in the same way as the civil rights of the negro, and on the ground of this dogma concerning the Jew's economic position.

Other exclusions derived therefrom also—social exclusions, and the program of reform which meant the assimilation of the Jew to his social environment, found itself completely inhibited and frustrated by the environment's rejection of this suicidal good-will. The reformer conceived that the Jew was to be a German or an Englishman or an Italian of the "Jewish persuasion," just as an Englishman might be of the Christian persuasion. The program failed, the conception was as barren as it was hopeful. The "emancipated" Jews felt, and still feel and resent their "disability" more intensely than before the emancipation. They became ashamed of their Jewish connection. They began to deny it, to hide it, if they could not destroy it. They became, in effect, amateur Gentiles, and the momentum of this becoming has been continuous and shows no sign of losing force or speed. It is, of course, a process of losing self-respect and dignity.

In Eastern Europe, conditions were different. The Jewry of the West were a few small communities, not more than two hundred thousand Jews in Germany, and many less in England, and less in France; none to be mentioned in Italy. The great mass of them were concentrated in the Pale, in Poland and Lithuania, on the boundary between Eastern and Western Europe. Conditions in the former region, compelled, under czarism, a restatement of the Jewish status, no longer in terms of religion, but in terms of economic and social functions. In the west it was found that religious conceptions could not hold at all in face of the progress of rationalism. Judaists in the very ministry itself developed into agnostics and atheists and the reform rabbis, who had engineered reform, soon found that they were losing the best of their young men and women. Social ambition or desire for higher standing in the state led to many conversions and to other features in the picture of reform as the deliquescence I have just designated. In Eastern Europe that problem expressed itself in a different way. There the great numbers of the Jews made it possible for the Jewish community as a whole to assimilate the new learning and make it a part of its own mind. In Western Europe the communities were too weak and too small. They were minorities of inferior culture amid majorities of superior culture. In Eastern Europe the Jews were culturally superior to their neighbors, and numerically self-sufficient. In what is called the Haskalah, the enlightenment, they underwent the readjustment which the communal absorption of the new mind of Europe meant. The Haskalah consists in the slow and steady absorption of the historic culture of Western Europe by the Jewish people until that becomes quite Jewish. The Jewish community did not lose its community character; it did not disintegrate. There took place, of course, a bitter quarrel about the absorption of this new learning, and physical conflicts and religious excommunications were not infrequent. The change was not made without a great struggle, but it was made. In its unfolding the Jewish community was the active, assimilating life, whereas in Western Europe, the Jewish community was the passive, assimilated matter.

The outcome of the Haskalah, which is the true reform, the actual reform of Jewish life in Eastern Europe, is the recovery of the idea of Jewish nationality on a secular and civil basis, as the peer of other European nationalities. Consequently, Jewish life has become for the community indefinitely more extensive than the Jewish religion; it has become an organic envelope and support for religion as

the body is for the lungs or the heart. In it religion is but
a part. It has remained *Jewish* life, but it has acquired a
completely secular dimension. This is to be observed in
the modern neo-Hebrew and Yiddish literature, in the development of secular theories of Jewish history, in the
organization of Jewish education on a secular basis, in the
rise and growth of Jewish art and music, in the complete
emergence of the Jewish mind in Yiddish and Hebrew
literature, in the reorganization of the community. The
non-Judaistic Jew, like the Bundist or Revolutionist in
Russia, is not cut off from his community by his non-
adherence to Judaism. In the reformed synagogue of
Western Europe, inability to agree with the reform rabbis
on Judaism is by rabbinic fiat self-elimination from the
Jewish community. In Eastern Europe, in a word, there
has been a reform as complete and drastic as the reform
in Western Europe, but in Eastern Europe the reform has
been creative and renovating. It has been performed by
an assimilation of the new elements to the old. In Western
Europe, it has cut off the old elements altogether. In consequence, Judaism among the Jews has become as Christianity among the Gentiles, a subordinate part of the
greater Jewish life.

VI

The name I prefer for this greater Jewish life is Hebraism. Judaism is only a part of Hebraism. Judaism is not
the whole of Jewish life. It is no longer, deplorable though
that may be, even at the center of Jewish life. The great
concerns of the Jewish people are the spiritual concerns
of all nationalities in Europe. They are the concerns of
international civilization. Religion is a part of those, but
only a part. In the great community of Jews the organization of life is not changed. In that community Jews still

"eat Kosher," but under a rationalized and secular law; their community organization continues and fulfils their historic tradition, but its sanction is no longer regarded as supernatural; is no longer the conception of a divinity working upon them from without; it is the conception of the people seeing itself, being conscious of itself, its beginnings, its growth and its direction, from within. It is the Hebraic spirit finding itself in the various institutions and problems of Jewish life as a whole, awake to the tasks and endeavors of the modern and secular world.

The problem of Judaism is at this point not any different from the problems of any other religion. It is the problem of saving itself, of keeping going in a setting which on the whole is secular, and promises to become more and more so. It is perfectly clear that the value of religion can be determined only by its bearing on the rest of life, and so far as the survival of Judaism is concerned, if Judaism is to survive at all, it can survive only as a functional component of this larger living complex we call Hebraism. Just as the nose or the arm can go on existing only so long as it is attached to the body, so alone can a religion go on existing. If you cut off Jewish religious life from the total complex of Jewish life, you cut it off from life. It has been so cut off in the reform synagogue, and that is why the generations of the reformed do not remain Judaists. The place of religion is within, not above or around, the social complex. Elsewhere, the sap of life either melts it or leaves it. Orthodoxy hence is stiffening, and is left, as the penalty for cutting off Judaism from the larger life which Jewry shares with all mankind, dry and brittle. Reform again is jellified and melting, as the penalty for cutting off Judaism from concrete and specific sources of its *particular* and Jewish being, for shattering its natural channel. If orthodoxy is a rocky barren, reform is a gas-breeding swamp. As mere religious sects, there is no healthy life in either.

The Haskalah movement represents not a middle way between these two extremes, but a third and altogether different way. Its history has emerged as an assimilation of the new material to the old vision. In a word, it designates the line of growth in Jewish life. In the Haskalah movement there began a natural readjustment of the organic Jewish community, the nationality, to its new life-conditions. By virtue of this readjustment Judaism can get its proper place in the co-ordination of things which compose the Jewish national life. For survival, Judaism is dependent on the continuance of the Jewish community-complex. Unless, however, this community-complex is thought of in historic terms, in terms of the Jewish spiritual individuality, of Jewish tradition, customs, history, growth, there is no place for Judaism. The place and function of Judaism in Jewish life is like the place and function of any religion in any national life. It is an item in that life; only an item, no matter how important, in a whole which is determined by the ethnic character of the people that live it, by their history, by their collective will and intent. These three factors define the total conditions of national life. Judaism, to survive, must fit among the other social elements somewhere in a Jewish national life. If it does not, it will, in the natural course of things, die. There exists, however, much uncertainty about the will and intent of the Jewish life. And so long as this remains, Judaism remains a problem. The problem of Judaism cannot be solved by itself. It requires to be treated as a part of the solution of the problem of the *Jewish people*.

1918

X

ZIONISM AND LIBERALISM

Mr. Morris Cohen delivering himself on Zionism, says he attacks, not Zionism the measure of relief, but Zionism the expression of a "nationalist philosophy." Ostensibly, it is this philosophy which horrifies Mr. Cohen. Now it happens that this philosophy is as widespread as civilization, that it permeates all peoples, particularly oppressed peoples; that it utters a state of mind and feeling basic to established as well as aspiring nationalities. Nor are Americans of the ruling class unendowed with it. Of course, like other philosophies, even "liberalism," it rests upon premises in nature and in human experience and aspiration which can be used to establish conclusions that are paranoia and fantasy. Such are the conclusions of Chamberlain's Teutonism and Katkoff's Slavism. But there is as little reason in identifying those with the normal "nationalist philosophy" of Zionism as there is in identifying Lloyd George, who is one of its defenders, with William Hohenzollern, or England with Germany, or a normal man with a lunatic. The Jewish nationality is only one among very many which has a program of regeneration and freedom resting upon the common normal nationalist philosophy. That Mr. Cohen should choose to pervert that one, rather than the program of any other—say of the Poles or Greeks or Italians, as he might, with better reason, do—is an unconscious admission of the truths envisaged in "nationalist philosophy" which even

111

liberals of Mr. Cohen's kind might profitably ponder.

To the contentions Mr. Cohen offers in support of his caricature of Zionism the facts compel a categorical denial. It is simply false that "Zionism rests on a nationalist philosophy which is a direct challenge to liberalism." The nationalist philosophy of Zionism is an extension of the assumptions of liberalism from the individual to the group. It antedated the "liberalism of the French Revolution" by a thousand years, and only changed, as Spinoza suggested that it might, from a religious to a political mode in consequence of that revolution. Of course, it is "anti-assimilationist." Pan-Germanism, pan-Slavism, and all the other panic movements are assimilationist. They refuse to minorities the right of association in communities of speech, of custom, tradition and culture according to their own lights and ways. They want to Germanize, Slavonize, Magyarize; and they have their echoes in America. Democracy is anti-assimilationist. It stands for the acknowledgment, the harmony and organization of group diversities in co-operative expansion of the common life, not for the assimilation of diversities into sameness. Zionism is anti-assimilationist because it is democratic, because it has enough faith in "the progress of the slow movement known as enlightenment," to apply its teachings to groups as well as to individuals. Had Mr. Cohen spoken from observation rather than passion, he would have known these things.

Through more than a millennium and a half the Jewish people were subject to disabilities, individual and collective, either because they were held to belong to an alien creed or because they were held to belong to a "foreign" nation or both. Liberation from these disabilities was conditional upon conversion, assimilation—both surrender of conscience and alienation from relatives, friends and community—that is, upon repudiating the essential rights of freedom of thought and of association. If enlightenment has meant anything at all, it has meant the progressive confirmation of these two rights. In the life of the peoples of Europe to assert these rights was to give concrete expression to "the cosmopolitan reason and enlightenment which overthrew mediævalism." The nationalism which is only another name for them was a development of, not a reaction against, the spirit of the French Revolution. It was that spirit which all over the continent of Europe fought both the imperialism of Napoleon and the oppression of the dynasts. Democracy and nationalism made up a single engine of liberalism; they were together against the oppressor. The prophet and philosopher of this nationalism is not Chamberlain, not Katkoff, but Mazzini, and the sum of his teaching might be uttered in a slight modification of the Declaration of Independence: all nationalities are created equal and endowed with certain inalienable rights; among these rights are life, liberty and the pursuit of happiness.

This is the whole Zionist ideology. Zionists have opposed it on the one hand to the clerics of the reformed synagogue who do not in fact "fundamentally accept the ideology of Chamberlain and Katkoff, but draw different conclusions," preaching the arrogant doctrine of the "chosen people" and the "mission of Israel," and on the other to the protagonists of this anti-Semitic ideology itself. To both the Zionists have said: "The Jews are a historic people among other peoples, neither better nor worse. They have their national qualities which their past attests and which afford some indication of the future. They are entitled equally with any other to express their qualities freely and autonomously as a group, making such contribution to the co-operative enterprise of

civilization as their qualities as a group promise." Nobody who has read Ruppin and Zollschan, who have met
the ethnological attack, nor the host of writers (whose
dean is Ah'ad Ha'am) who have met the religious and
cultural attack, could have failed to know this, nor to
recognize the true liberalism of which it is an extension.

For the naturalistic cosmopolitanism of the eighteenth
century analyzed the living groupings of mankind into
abstract individuals—"natural" men; while the economic
internationalism of the nineteenth analyzed it into equally
abstract individuals—"economic" men: laborers, capitalists. Both failed to see that individuality was not congenital but achieved, and that all men depend in their
beginnings on a society which is a *natio* before it is anything else. Its power in the history of democratic times,
against the appeal of all other sorts of associations,
should have opened their eyes, but did not. It cannot be
disposed of merely by refutation of absurd dialectic aber-
ration or eugenic claims based on it. Whether races or
nationalities are of "pure" breed or not, they exist as associations deriving from a real or credited predominant
inheritance, an intimate sameness of background, tradition, custom and aspiration. Genuine liberalism requires
for them the same freedom of development and expression
as for the individual. Indeed, in requiring it for the individual, it must necessarily require it for them. They are
the essential reservoirs of individuality. This is why seven,
I think, of the eight men whom Mr. Cohen names have
immediately behind them the highly integrated, autonomous and exclusive life of the ghetto. Zionism might be
described as aiming to conserve and strengthen, under far
more favorable than ghetto conditions, the values of such
a type of reservoir.

For the sources of cultures are in those types, and no-

where else. Thus, the language of the Roman conqueror
was absorbed by the Spanish and Portuguese no less than
by the French. It underlies Italian also. But what mankind prizes in the spirits and literatures of these peoples
is just that diversity which comes from Latin having been
used by peoples of different breeds, traditions and habits.
Perhaps Mr. Cohen's liberalism would have been satisfied
with a universal Latinity. Mediæval religious imperialism
and scholastic pedantry did their best to enforce that.
Nevertheless, true liberals do not regret that Dante's
Italian, and Cervantes's Spanish and Camoëns's Portuguese exist beside Molière's French and St. Thomas's
Latin. They know that the alternative to diversity of
cultures is cultural imperialism, of which, modernly, the
Prussians have illustrated the possibilities both in pretension and in theory. They have their imitators, and the Jews
have suffered for their rejection of such imperialism from
ancient times to the present day. It is slander to attribute
to the Zionists anything beyond the wish for international
service through national freedom.

II

And why should they not believe that this service and
freedom may best come in Palestine? The idea that
Palestine is the Jewish land and the Jews are the Palestinian people is a part of the two thousands years' continuous tradition of Europe. The "return to Jerusalem"
is the very heart of the tradition of Jewry over the same
period, of the governance of their lives and of their power
to survive the immolations they were forced to undergo.
But, dogmatizes Mr. Cohen, "nationalistic Zionism demands not complete individual liberty for the Jew but
group autonomy." Then he deduces, via an irresponsible
editorial from a defunct Jewish paper that this "must nec-

essarily" mean conscription of conscience by a tribal religion, an illiberal control of life, the ignoring of "the rights of the vast non-Jewish population of Palestine."

Nothing could be falser. Nationalistic Zionism demands not only group autonomy, but complete individual liberty for the Jew *as Jew*. It points to the fact that what Mr. Cohen calls enlightenment has failed—and evidently Mr. Cohen wants it to persist in this failure—because it has offered the Jew complete individual liberty on condition that he cease being a Jew. Zionism extends the principle of enlightenment by requiring for the Jew complete individual liberty not only as an abstract "human being" of ambiguous nationality, but also as a Jew. Zionism asserts the principle of freedom of association. Perhaps the most dramatic exemplification of it on record came at the American Jewish Congress in Philadelphia, where duly elected representatives of all Jewish parties in America assumed responsibility for the Zionist program. Upon the demand of the "red" section of the Congress an unscheduled speaker was added to the program. In the course of his address he assaulted orthodoxy in such a way as bitterly to offend the orthodox, who interrupted him. They permitted him to conclude on the representation of one of their own party that their pride had always been toleration of differences. I doubt whether other churches, be they traditional or radical, can produce a similar instance. And this was a responsible and representative action; but Mr. Cohen calls attention to an irresponsible and unrepresentative writer. Again, had Mr. Cohen been truly moved by a liberal spirit in regard to Zionism he would have set against the "must necessarily" of his own irresponsible inferences the record of the responsible organization accomplishment. I refer to the subjoined program of reconstruction unanimously adopted by the Zionist organization at its last convention and assented to by the Zionists of the world:

"The recent declarations of Great Britain, France, Italy, and others of the Allied democratic states have established the public recognition of the Jewish national home as an international fact.

"Therefore we desire to affirm anew the principles which have guided the Zionist movement since its inception. . . .

"First: Political and civil equality irrespective of race, sex or faith of all the inhabitants of the land.

"Second: To insure in the Jewish national home in Palestine equality of opportunity we favor a policy which, with due regard to existing rights, shall tend to establish the ownership and control of the land and of all natural resources and of all public utilities by the whole people.

"Third: All land, owned or controlled by the whole people, should be leased on such conditions as will insure the fullest opportunity for development and continuity of possession.

"Fourth: The cooperative principle should be applied so far as feasible in the organization of all agricultural, industrial, commercial and financial undertakings.

"Fifth: The fiscal policy should be framed so as to protect the people from the evils of land speculation and from every other form of financial oppression.

"Sixth: The system of free public instruction which is to be established should embrace all grades and departments of education.

"Seventh: The medium of public instruction shall be Hebrew, the national language of the Jewish people."

The Zionists obviously do not contemplate at any point the program Mr. Cohen so liberally maps out for them. But Mr. Cohen infers that unless they do, "a

Jewish Palestine would soon lose its very reason for existence." The Zionists are confident enough to leave this to the decision of events. The homeland they seek to establish for the Jews in Palestine has the endorsement of both the governments and the peoples of the Allied democracies. It has their endorsement because they do believe that it will solve the Jewish problem, solve it precisely because it will facilitate the adjustment of "the members of a certain historic group" to the majorities among whom they live. It will do this because it will create the prerequisite thereto, and the prerequisite to the liberation of the individual is the liberation of the group to which he by birth belongs. As a consequence of the disfranchisement of the Jewish people as such, a millennium and a half ago, the position of the individual Jew became civically ambiguous, particularly in Eastern Europe. He was part of an *imperium in impero*, at one and the same time both a subject and not a subject of Russia, Roumania, Poland, Germany or France. He was without an explicit or unmistakable center of reference, and again and again this situation was maliciously used to impugn his loyalties and allegiances. The creation of the homeland in Palestine will restore the Jewish people as such to the status of equality with other peoples which Christian Europe had robbed them of. It will thus clear up the ambiguity of the status of the individual Jew. It will enable Mr. Cohen or any other to say without being doubted: "I do belong with those people there" or "I do not belong with those people there," as does the Frenchman, Pole or Italian. If nationality does not constitute a problem for these migrants as for the Jews, it is because actual majorities of them do inhabit politically definite areas generally acknowledged to be their homelands. Their status is not ambiguous. The Jew in America or elsewhere will not be free to "adjust himself harmoniously" with the non-Jew until he also becomes unambiguous. The re-establishment of the Jewish homeland will make it so and it is thus an essential element in the "harmonious adjustment of the Jew to American life."

This life, just in so far as it has been liberal and liberating, has formed the dynamics and inspiration of the effort of American Jews in behalf of Zion, as it has of other Europe-born groups in behalf of collective freedom and collective self-expression in their ancestral lands. This is a freedom which, for good or evil, they cannot attain and should not seek in America. Their utmost here is, as Mr. Cohen points out, to contribute their own past experience to the dominant cultural tradition and compenetrate their old community with the others which have their habitation in the new place. The contribution, consequently, which the Jews or any other non-English peoples are likely in America to make to civilization is not Polish, nor French, nor German, nor Jewish, but American.

Only in cases where the Jewish community can survive and grow organically as Jewish can the Jews' contribution to civilization be Jewish. The French or English or Italian contributions to civilization come from France and England and Italy, not from America. For obvious reasons each is more purely and essentially that and nothing else in the home country which is a living individuality of its particular kind, absorbing and assimilating influences from the whole world and making them over into the substance of its own flesh and spirit. What is achieved is a cause for pride and distinction in its children elsewhere, as our French alliances and Spanish societies and so on attest. Now it is a curious sort of liberalism which will concede this situation for the peoples mentioned and not for the Jews. Or, for that matter, for the negroes. If the arguments for Palestine find their parallel on behalf of Liberia they do so no less on behalf of England and France and Germany and Italy and Russia.

In sum: Liberalism, according to Mr. Cohen, would require a Jew or an Englishman or Frenchman to owe allegiance to and take pride in any nationality but his own. Similarly it might require a man to love any woman but his wife. What Mr. Cohen calls liberalism turns out, under examination, to be very difficult to distinguish in its implications from Prussianism or cultural imperialism. What he calls tribalism turns out to be a perverse name for what in the political tradition of Europe and the aspiration of peoples has usually been called democracy. Of this tradition and aspiration Zionism is a part. It conceives human society as a democratic co-operative organization of nationalities, no less than of other forms of the associations of men in the endeavor after life, liberty and happiness, and it claims for the Jews opportunity and security in this type of association. It is the liberal world which acknowledges and assists this claim.

1919

XI

REALISTIC ZIONISM

"We want," the editor of the *Survey* wrote in the course of the letter asking for this essay, "the economic and social background of this whole movement. In other words, I think there are a lot of people today who still are not quite clear as to what Zionism really means."

The sentences are symptomatic. They could at this time hardly have been written with regard to the nationalist endeavor of the Irish, the Poles, the Czecho-Slovaks, or any other of the lesser peoples of Europe whom the Great War has liberated or stimulated to greater efforts toward freedom. The nationalism of the Jews, like so many other matters touching them equally with other peoples, is felt, for the most part unconsciously, to be somewhat different, and the question gets raised far more among the lettered than the unlettered classes, as to what it "really means."

Now this difference truly exists, and the confusion as to what anything pertaining to the Jews "really means" is not ungrounded. It is asserted by the Jews no less than by the Christians and it is summed up in a popular dictum that the Jews are a "peculiar people." The dictum has been made the point of departure for the fabrication by both Jews and their enemies of a great deal of mythological anthropology and sociology and history and religion, designed to belittle or to glorify them, according to the prejudices of the fabricators. The ridiculous forgeries which Mr. Henry Ford has known how to employ are examples of the one, and the hardly less ridiculous formulations of "the mission of Israel" by Jewish theological pundits are examples of the other. Both are postulated upon the felt difference or peculiarity of the Jews. Both assume that this difference or peculiarity is inherent, an essential element in the original nature of the Jewish people.

As a matter of fact, it is nothing of the sort. It is an acquired and secondary quality. It attaints the Jew as infection from his Christian environment. In Christian countries with civilized religious organizations and liberal socio-political institutions, the infection comes from the influence of the teachings and tradition of the cultus upon the cultural milieu. In uncivilized Christian countries with backward religious and socio-political institutions the infection is universal and endemic, the Jew is made and kept different by his formal or legal status under the fundamental law of the land as well as by the sentiment and practical attitude of his Christian neighbors. To them, wherever they are, and whether they have even seen a Jew or not, the word "Jew" evokes a different motor set and emotional tone from the word "Pole" or "Armenian" or "Slovak," or other such words, and a different complex of associations, among which Palestine is one, and prominently one. The difference is something additive, and not pleasant. It derives from the Christian tradition, both the idealogical tradition and the institutional tradition.

In this tradition the position of the Jew is determined by his peculiar rôle in the drama of salvation. His career in this drama begins as that of "the chosen people"; it ends as that of the rejected people. Objects of divine election, God the Father sends his only-begotten Son to be incarnated among the Jews as the Saviour of mankind from the consequences of the sin of Adam. But the Jews reject the Saviour and crucify him, and are for this reason themselves rejected from the heavenly favor and the fellowship of salvation, banished from their homeland Palestine to live dispersed among the nations as outcasts and outlaws, until such time as the second coming of Christ as the Paraclete. When, in the fourth century, Christianism was adopted as the state religion, this ideology was given literal effect by the official outlawing of the Jewish people from citizenship in the Roman Empire. Until the beginning of the nineteenth century such was their position throughout Europe—without rights, without status, without security or freedom, at the mercy of any wind of doctrine or passion that blew among the rulers and masses of the hemisphere. The more civilized of the Christian states have, since that time, admitted the Jews distributively to legal or formal equality of status as citizens.

But the Jews are a historic community, and "Jew" is a collective and not a singular term; it stands for a group and membership in a group. When applied to any individual it is accompanied by an automatic and mostly unconscious emotional attitude and motor set, established by the preconceptions of the cult absorbed in childhood. And these, legal or formal equality cannot touch; their alteration would require a basic alteration of the religious tradition and its transmission. That such an alteration has been slowly taking place since the Protestant Reformation is a commonplace of cultural history. But it has been far from significant or considerable enough to prevent the survival of the preconceptions transmitted in childhood as unconscious determinants of the feeling and conduct of the mature adult, or to save the Jew from the practical disabilities and varied limitations of the relationships they impose on the daily life. The peculiar interest, for example, in Mr. Henry Ford's silly "Protocols" rests directly upon them.

These disabilities and limitations, persistent in varying intensities for a millennium and a half, must needs have had their inevitable effect on the Jewish psyche. For one thing, they deprived the Jews of the varied overt civil life which is necessary to the economy of any healthy group; they confined creative impulse, which in the normal free community expresses itself in the total complex of social and institutional activities, to a very few and these, outlawed, economic activities; and to religion and the disciplines—particularly to the learning—associated with religion. For another, they set and kept—and this condition obtains today—the daily life of the great majority of the Jews under the dominion of fear, and they imposed a specific and generalized inferiority of which they compelled public acknowledgment in garb and conduct. As a consequence, the observed Jewish behavior in the Christian social setting revealed habits of response evoked and established by such causes—habits observable in any persecuted or repressed people: the Irish for example, or the Armenians, or the Poles or Jugoslavs.

The unobserved, "inner," or deep spiritual, life of the Jews again, their imaginative or "ideal," religious and cultural life, became essentially compensatory—that is, it became a correction in imagination of the evils and deficiencies of reality. Imposed exoteric inferiority was compensated for by the assumption of an esoteric superiority on the ground of divine perference: "the chosen people" is a comforting inward defense against actual degradation. Fear was compensated for by scorn, public shame by private pride. The whole complex of instincts, impulses and interests which the Jewish position in the Christian world repressed was compensated for by the image of an ideal commonwealth in Palestine, to which the Jews were to be restored by the supernatural intervention of Messiah the son of David. Zion became the mystic symbol of the enablement of all the felt disabilities, the release of all the unnatural repressions, the restoration of the Jewish people to freedom and health. The hope of this restoration was an ancient one. It is on record in the Bible and elsewhere as the natural aspiration of a conquered and subject people to regain their freedom and autonomy. Through half the first millennium of the Christian era it remained secular and natural, and found expression in a series of military and economic endeavors to realize it. Then in proportion as the position of the Jews in Europe grew more and more unhappy and hopeless it acquired supernatural mystical elements, until finally it became the magic core of salvation, a dreamworld of refuge and consolation from the terrible realities that beset the Jews.

II

The idea of the restoration of the Jews to Zion, of the restoration of Zion to the Jews, thus became the saving fact in the life of the Jewish community in Europe. It enabled them to endure and to survive. It was the integrating factor in the group psyche and saved it from going to pieces in madness and despair. And it was as familiar and commonplace to Christianity as it was precious to Judaism. The time came, however, when Europe began to undergo secularization. The position of the Christian cult began to shift from the center of European life to its periphery. A new economy, generating new ideas about the structure and significance of the universe, the nature and destiny of man, the sanction and purposes of government, whether ecclesiastical or secular, finally emerged in the social upheaval of the French revolution, with its maxim "Libery, Equality, Fraternity." The underlying preconceptions of this maxim—which is purely compensatory—were that men are by nature equal—and equal was made synonymous with similar, so that their differences became secondary, imposed by church and state for their own advantage, the effect merely of the repressions of men's similarities.

In the course of time these preconceptions got applied by the Christians to the Jews and by the Jews to themselves. The application eventuated in a slow, uneven and contrasted secularization of the Jewish psyche: contrasted West and East. In the West it took shape as "Reform Judaism." Reform Judaism reverses the mediæval position. In that, the spontaneous group similarities between Jews and their neighbors were repressed intentionally by their neighbors. In reform Judaism, the spontaneous group differences between Jews and their neighbors are intentionally repressed by the Jews: Jews become, not Christians, but amateur Gentiles; Frenchmen, Germans, Russians or Englishmen "of the Mosaic persuasion." In the East, where the overwhelming majority of the Jews still live, the secularization was not intentional. It followed the same line as the Renaissance in Christian Europe, and developed during the nineteenth century by contagion and absorption from the West European countries. Its upshot was the recovery, by the perennial hope of the restoration of the Jews to Zion of something of its ancient *secular* status; its reconversion from a compensatory ideal to rest in into a practical program to effectuate.

The recovery and reconversion have never been quite complete. The modern position of the Jewish people in the east of Europe has been too like their mediæval position to permit of that. As a nationalist movement, hence, Zionism is in one sense the most ancient, in another the latest, of the nationalisms which, awakened by the French Revolution, dominated the socio-political history of Europe during the nineteenth century and are likely to dominate it for another hundred years. Its philosophy is like the philosophy of all nationalisms to which Mazzini has given classical expression.

But there is an additional dimension to the Jewish nationalism which is called Zionism—a dimension among the imponderables of the mind. It involves an alteration in the psychology of the Jew as a persecuted people, quite divergent from that aimed at by reform Judaism. The latter, while repressing all other differences between Jews and their neighbors, retains and re-interprets those which establish the compensatory idea of Jewish superiority: the Jews, it holds, are a chosen people, with a religious mission in the world, dispersed over it as "world priests"; and its protagonists fear and resent any acknowledgment of Jewish nationality under the law of nations as a menace to their actual status of comfort and their compensating superiority complex. They hence denounce Zionism and suffer from what the London *Times* has called an "imaginative nervousness" about the effects to them of its realization. The old Zionists, on the other hand, while demanding the equality of freedom for the social expression of the whole Jewish psyche, similarities and differences alike, cling still to the compensatory ideology of the religious past: Palestine and life in Palestine are endowed with perfections that pertain to Utopia, so that it becomes difficult or well-nigh impossible to effect among the Zionist masses a realistic apprehension of the problem in Palestine.

Now this state of things is abnormal. It is a symptom

that the prevailing psychology of both the well-to-do "assimilated" Jews of the West and the disinherited and suffering nationalist Jews of Eastern Europe has remained the psychology of a persecuted people, motivated by fear and an inferiority complex. It may be manifested in the shrill apprehensiveness of a type like Henry Morgenthau or the passionate self-confidence of a type like Schmarja Levin: the same sub- or semi-conscious trends underlie both. It is quite different from the normal group psyche of a people whose security and freedom are so commonplace, so natural, as to be as unconscious as breathing in a healthy man. And it is, for the reasons already indicated, a more complicated abnormality of consciousness and behavior than that which pertains to oppressed Christian nationalities—the Irish, for example, or the Poles, or the Armenians. From the point of view of the health of society, of the whole of society, the essential need is to abolish the causes of this abnormal situation: causes which, like a focal infection in the organism, keep generating strains and maladjustments and functional disturbances throughout the whole body politic, Christians and Jews alike. Zionism, in the considered opinion of the most normal sections of the Jewish community, and of the wisest and most sophisticated statesmanship of the Christian world, is the instrument which will most aid to restore this normality in the case of the Jews. As Mr. Justice Brandeis wrote in 1915:

> Enlightened countries grant to the individuals equality before the law: but they fail still to recognize the equality of whole peoples or nationalities. We seek to protect as individuals those constituting a minority, but we fail to realize that protection cannot be complete unless group equality is also recog-

nized. . . . (The Zionists seek this recognition in their acknowledged homeland, Palestine.) They believe that there only can Jewish life be fully protected from the forces of disintegration; that there only can the Jewish spirit reach its full and natural development; and that by securing for the Jews who wish to settle in Palestine the opportunity to do so, not only those Jews, but all other Jews will be benefited and that the long perplexing Jewish problem will, at last, find solution.

And as Mr. A. J. Balfour wrote in 1918:

Everything which assimilates the national and international status of the Jews to that of other races ought to mitigate what remains of ancient antipathies: and evidently this assimilation would be promoted by giving them that which all other nations possess: a local habitation and a national home.

The local habitation and the national home are now designated and fixed by international agreement and the law of nations. The general effect of the Balfour Declaration, and the Treaty of San Remo which incorporated it, upon Jews of all classes has been, regardless of their former attitude to Zionism, somewhat of gratulation and gratitude, much of awakening responsibility: the universal anxiety and regret which the split between the American and the European leaders caused is evidence, no less than the offers of co-operation from the most diversified sections of the world's Jewish community.

The realization that the Treaty of San Remo created an unprecedented situation for the Jewish people, that it offered at once an opportunity and a challenge was apparent everywhere, except among the leaders of the World

Zionist Organization. The new condition and its new problems found them altogether unprepared. It was entirely without precedent in their experience. That experience had been overwhelmingly on the level of propaganda, not administration. Its force and background had been the only partially secularized love of Zion of the great Jewish masses, and this love had for too long found itself not merely used, but used up, in the diplomatic manipulations of persons, in phrasemaking and in almsgiving. The administration of the Zionist institutions, whether in Europe or Palestine or America had had the same character. It was like the administration of charities in the pre-scientific era.

Moreover, the self-regarding sentiments, the feelings of personal destiny and personal worth, and in a good many cases, the livelihoods of a great many of these leaders were bound up in intricate and complex ways with this propaganda organization. Throughout the twenty-five years of its existence their habits of thought and action in relation to it had become fixed and rigid, their procedures inevitably routinal. It was not to be expected that they would be able, even under the most critical circumstances, to alter them, any more than Dmowski or other European politicans in or out of office were able to alter theirs. And during the war, alteration was neither possible nor desirable. The problem was a diplomatic and an educational problem, and the old organization and old leadership were adequate enough to work at it. But the Treaty of San Remo solved the problem. It realized the "Basle Program." It gave public guarantees under international law that Palestine would be restored as the national home of the Jewish people. It put a period to the preliminary phase of Zionist endeavor. It crowned the old Zionism with success, and it established conditions the meeting of which required a new Zionism, of a radically different character from the old.

III

But for one circumstance, the Zionists might have blundered along like the Poles, and the Letts, and the Lithuanians and the others, with very much greater risk, of course, of frittering away their dearly-gained opportunity; indeed, on the record, with the certainty of so doing. The circumstance was the assumption, in 1914, of the active leadership of the movement in the United States by Mr. (now Justice) Louis D. Brandeis, and the participation of such men as Judge Julian W. Mack, Mr. Bernard Flexner, Prof. Felix Frankfurter, Mr. Nathan Straus, among many others, in the administrative responsibility. This circumstance, on the record, made the determining difference between success and failure in the old Zionism. It converted the Zionist movement in the United States from a ghetto incident into the largest and most effective Jewish organization in the land. It introduced method and responsibility into the administrative organs of the movement. It enabled the raising of enough money to carry out the task of diplomatic work and of propaganda and education on the scale necessitated by the war, and to maintain the Jewish institutions in Palestine. Particularly it tended to shift the Jewish thinking about Palestine from the compensatory to the objective and realistic level.

This last tendency, which is obviously most important, gathered, however, very little momentum. There were many reasons for this—the great resistance of immemorial tradition and habit; the administrative secrecy necessitated by war conditions; the profound differences of psychology between the new leadership and the old Zionists arising from differences in training, experience, and outlook; and the marked class-resentment which these differences generated among the Yiddish-speaking masses and their journalist spokesmen. This feeling grew more intense from the time of the Armistice on. It was fanned from Europe, for the contacts established there between the American and European leaders led, in a period of two years, to discovery by the Americans of administrative waste and incompetency, fiduciary irresponsibility and political thimblerigging of which they demanded correction, and correction of which was in the nature of things impossible. The Americans were merely denounced for their lack of idealism, were sneered at as materialists, as "business-Zionists," and were steadily undermined with their constituencies.

When finally the Zionist chief, Dr. Weizmann, and his associates came to the United States, he was ready with a number of false issues and focalizing phrases. The Americans were accused of disloyalty to the world organization, of holding to a Zionist "Monroe Doctrine," of "defeatism." The "Keren Hayesod" or Foundation Fund, which the Americans denounced as a usurpation of the authority of the World Zionist Congress and a serious economic blunder, was used as the integrating formula for all the streams of mass sentiment. The publication of a few of the more important items of the irregularities in London and Palestine, which the Americans had until then kept silent about, made no difference. They simply strengthened the barrier of feeling which had been erected between the mass and the American leaders. At the convention in Cleveland these leaders were repudiated; Dr. Weizmann and his associated propangandists were confirmed in their hold on the Zionist organization. In the nature of things that and not the problem in Palestine is their primary concern; old Zionists they were, and old Zionists they cannot help remaining.

That the realistic Americans should dissociate themselves from all responsibility for them and their policies was inevitable. That they should plan out a new program of work, relevant to the specific problems set by the economic and social character of Palestine and the Jews was equally inevitable. For there are involved in the concrete undertakings they plan not only the gradual solution of the Jewish problem by the upbuilding of the Jewish homeland but the relief and rehabilitation of hundreds of thousands of Jews whom the war has reduced to the state of nomads, who are driven from frontier to frontier in Central Europe and who have a *right* of refuge, under international guarantees, only in Palestine. There are in the Ukraine half a million homeless Jewish children of whom more than 200,000 are orphans, who have no hope to grow by, save, perhaps, in Palestine. To meet immediate problems such as these, politics and propaganda are irrelevant; economic operations are crucial. As Mr. Justice Brandeis had already said in July, 1920, to the American delegates at the London Conference: "The political question is important hereafter, but to my mind practically the whole of politics is to proceed efficiently in the building up of Palestine. That is the only political act . . . which can effectively produce the result and make success instead of failure of our opportunity."

And this is the heart of the aspiration and program of the New Zionism. To render it efficacious, a conference was held in Pittsburgh, in July of this year, under the chairmanship of Judge Mack, in which 135 persons from all parts of the United States participated. This conference unanimously adopted the following resolution, and subscribed $218,000 of the $250,000 required for the first enterprise, to be paid within thirty days:

Whereas, The general objective, as means for development of the Jewish National Home, is outlined in the program of the Buffalo convention; and

Whereas, The upbuilding of the Jewish National Home cries out for immediate economic action on as large a scale as possible, to facilitate "The early settlement in Palestine of a preponderating body of self-supporting Jews," and

Whereas, Many of the operations proposed in the Buffalo program are now being undertaken by existing agencies; and competition, as well as duplication, must be avoided; and

Whereas, There remains to be done an unlimited amount of concrete economic work which may provide permanent means of livelihood for increasing numbers; and thus assist in the establishment of that indispensable, sound, economic foundation on which will be built the Jewish commonwealth which will embody our cherished ideals;

The committee on immediate economic enterprise and development of Palestine, begs to report its approval of the following for discussion and action:

1. That this conference undertake a series of enterprises through a Palestine Development Council.

2. That these enterprises shall be undertaken in the following order, so far as practical:

a. A wholesale supplies enterprise, as an instrument for supplying the industrial, agricultural and merchandising needs of the Jewish settlement in Palestine.

b. A house building construction enterprise.

c. A building and loan association to assist financing of home building requirements.

d. An industrial building and equipment fund.

e. An agricultural equipment fund.

3. That the plans of organization and details of the enterprises be determined by the Palestine development council.

4. That the organization should proceed from one concrete undertaking to another, step by step.

5. That the capital requirements for the enterprises undertaken, which shall each be undertaken as separate and distinct entities, shall be determined by the Palestine Development Council.

6. That the raising of the necessary capital for the various specific enterprises may be allotted in the discretion of the council to various cities, as particular objectives for the various respective cities.

7. That Palestinians are to be included in the management and operation of the enterprises, as far as possible.

8. The cooperative principle shall be applied in all enterprises as far as practicable. This includes the principle that profits shall be limited to a reasonable return on the investment; and that Palestinians may purchase shares of stock from any stockholder at any time at par so that untimately control and operation shall pass into the hands of Palestinian Jews and the corporation or enterprise shall become or shall be part of a cooperative society.

9. It is understood that the enterprises contemplated shall involve a capitalization in the aggregate of not less than $5,000,000. It is recommended that the authorized capital of the cooperative wholesale supply society be $1,000,000. The figure of $5,000,-

000 mentioned is not suggested as a goal or limit, but as a minimum. Contemplation of future activities should, however, not interfere with immediate action and operation should be commenced by the management as soon as possible. It is supposed that, in the discretion of the management, the cooperative whole-sale supply society may commence operations as soon as $250,000 is raised.

Under this resolution there has been erected the Palestine Development Council with Mr. Justice Brandeis as honorary chairman and Judge Julian Mack as chairman. As the report puts it:

> The purpose of the Palestine Development Council will be to undertake specific social-economic enterprises which will facilitate the early settlement in Palestine of a preponderating body of self-supporting Jews. The sole purpose of the council will be social-economic, not political. Its aim will be to assist in the upbuilding of a Jewish Palestine and to supplement, not interfere with, the efforts of others working toward a common end.
>
> The council will place primary emphasis in all its work upon the creation of a self-supporting economic life. Its object will be to help the Palestinians to help themselves: not to give them charity. The council will encourage and assist cooperative enterprises in Palestine. It is planned that the undertakings sponsored by the council will ultimately be purchased and directed by .Palestinian cooperatives."

Such are the program and the form of organization which, it has been decided, are likely to prove most effective in the development of the New Zionism. In this Zionism the compensatory interest in Palestine has quite given way to the objective and realistic interest; the magniloquent all-embracing project, to the itemized sequence of specific enterprises specifically undertaken. As compared with the character of the Keren Hayesod, it is modest, sober, limited. But on the record, only in proportion as these qualities prevail is success probable.

1921

XII

THE ROOTS OF ANTI-SEMITISM

There is today not a Christian country in the world without its modicum of anti-Semitism. This communal passion obtains, indeed, wherever Christianity has reached. Christian sectaries in China or Japan, in India or Arabia participate in it no less than Christian sectaries in Germany or Hungary, in Russia or in the United States, and suffuse the convert with its nazarene contagion. It is present regardless of contrary attitudes, contradictory interests, opposed ideals. It appears in the most unexpected quarters and in the most varied and complicating forms. It justifies itself by the most antagonistic reasons, and it passes from one to another, from any to all, from all to any with the somnambulistic heedlessness of a sleep-walker. Its basis is an emotion. Its origin is a gospel. Its biography is a sequence of rationalizations in which the emotion seeks a publicly acceptable symbol. Its origin, nature, and present behavior present one of the most ironic and revealing chapters in the picaresque tale which makes up the history of the European mind.

The nearer background of present-day anti-Semitism is, of course, the Great War. The soil and matrix of its current forms are the passions which were the life of the war and which did not die when the war ended.

War and battle are acute crises in the life of man. The body is regimented, the spirit is crowded and cornered. Action loses its civilized delicacies, feeling its finenesses.

Against surrounding, imminent, ever-nearing death a great anger develops, and a greater fear. The nice balances of peace-time habits break down. Inhibitions break down. Action and feeling become the simple elemental drives and sensibilities of the beast; behavior falls into primary and primitive patterns of defense and offense; thought becomes simplified and infantile.

A condition ensues which has its varieties but the living urge of which is always a dynamic fear, the same in all cases of it. As manifested in individuals this condition has gone by the generic name *shell-shock*. But social groups also are capable of undergoing fundamental disturbances whose animating source is fear and whose compensating emotion is anger. The collective fear projects itself upon the enemy. The enemy becomes really a symbol of the fear he evokes. The deeper the fear, the more "evil" the enemy. This view of the enemy becomes altogether independent of the facts in the case; the emotion generates its "facts" for itself. Hence the removal or disappearance of the outward cause or occasion for the emotion does not mean the immediate or even quick subsidence of the emotion itself. It grows by what it feeds on, even when it feeds on itself. So the removal, by the peace, of Germany as the evoking occasion of the emotion did not destroy the emotion. It survived and incarnated itself in a new symbol. This new symbol was bolshevism. The Bolshevists, the world over, replaced the Germans as the incarnation of ultimacies in evil, and a *Walpurgisnacht* of the cruelties of fear ensued from Viborg to Naples, from Moscow to Washington.

In the course of time Bolshevism lost its power as a channel for expression of the war emotion. But new sources of nourishment discovered themselves. Europe had begun to disintegrate. The institutional life of states, their industry, their commerce, their agriculture, their education, and very obviously their governments, were cracked at their foundations and crumbling in their super-structures. If the war emotion was a basic fear focalized by the enemy, the emotion of the peace was the same fear nourished by the disintegration of the customary insti-tutional supports of private life. The peace was a more radical case of community "shell-shock." The community began to fight illusions. One such battle with illusion is anti-Semitism.

Anti-Semitism is a chronic aspect of Christian history. It becomes acute during social crises and subsides in prosperity. The course it runs begins usually at some point of social disturbance where the cause is remote and not known and the distressful emotion is strong.* The Jews are then declared to be the hidden cause, and the emotion is enchanneled by and projected upon this sym-bol. Although there have been times when the common people, led usually by a Christian priest or monk, have been the initiators of anti-Semitic manifestations, the more customary source has been some disturbed or dis-located beneficiary of social privilege. Anti-Semitism has served very largely as an instrument of the upper classes. Its history in Central Europe during the last four years —from Poland to Roumania—its history in the United States, from Henry Ford to Lawrence Lowell and the Ku Klux Klan, are not exceptions. The obscene tale of the making, the dissemination, the emotional elaboration of the burlesqueries called the Protocols of the Elders of Zion reveal the frightened snarl and melodramatic strut of professional anti-Semites, scattered by political up-

* Thus the economic crisis of 1930–31 renewed it in an even intenser mode all over the continent of Europe.

heaval from all the scrapheaps of privilege of Europe. The matter of interest is not, however, that this nonsense was invented, but that being nonsense it should so readily, so almost inevitably, serve to integrate social fear and malaise. Why are the Jews the perennial devil of the piece?

The answer lies in the Christian religion itself, in the status which Christianity assigns to the Jews and the burden it sets and binds upon them. The answer lies in the rôle which Christian teaching plays in the make-up of the Western mind.

In broad outline, this teaching has for all sects an identical content, which may be called the Drama or Epic of Salvation. It tells of a first man created perfect and sinless, to dwell forever in the bucolic bliss of Eden. This first man was endowed with free will, and through the solicitation of the first woman exercised it, bringing "death into the world and all our woe." For God is just, and man's first disobedience merited no less than eternal death. But God is also merciful, and his mercy tempered his justice. The latter should be satisfied and yet man be saved. To this end it was preordained that a certain group of the human family should be chosen, under covenant, for especial communion with God; that among the descendants of this family God should send his only-begotten son to be born, to live poorly, and to die ignominiously upon the cross, a vicarious atonement for Adam's original sin, to be buried and on the third day to rise again and take his place in heaven upon the right hand of God. Then all those who believe this tale and accept this atonement will be saved from the consequences of Adam's sin. All those who do not believe and refuse the atonement will be damned. By the incarnation, crucifixion, and resurrection the world became divided into a congregation of the saved and a congregation of the damned.

The fortunate vessels of God's mercy which was to temper his justice were the Jews. They were the original chosen people. To them God revealed himself, his law, his purposes. Their history is signalized by manifestations of divine favor. As one of them, finally, the Savior became flesh and dwelt on earth as man.

But the Jews, instead of believing the tale of the Savior, repudiated it. Instead of accepting the atonement, they rejected it. They were made the instruments of his passion and death. Thereupon God's justice manifested itself anew. The old covenant was superseded by a new one, the old testament by a new. Divine favor was withdrawn from the Jews. The Chosen People became the Rejected People. From the crucifixion to the time of the Second Coming, they are doomed to live outside the fellowship of the saved, outcasts and outlaws, the brand of a sort of cosmic Cain upon their brows, their hands against every man's, every man's against them.

In the Christian system, then, the Jews are assigned a central and dramatic status. They are the villains of the Drama of Salvation. The gospel in which they so figure was carried to the farthermost corner of the European world. It became a part of the cultural inheritance of all the races of Europe, imparted equally to peer and to peasant. Nowhere in Europe could there be a village to whose inhabitants the word "Jew" did not denote the Rejected People who had once been chosen, who had denied the Savior and crucified him, who were thus the enemies of God and of mankind. Whatever else the masses and classes of Europe might not know, the nature and destiny of the Jew they knew. Most of them lived and died without ever exchanging a word with one of the race, but to all of them the word "Jew" was full of evil meaning. This meaning derived from no concrete experience with Jews. It was simply an emotional reaction to their name in the tale—a reaction that might vary from discomfort, repulsion, or malaise to flaming hatred. It was a reaction established in early childhood through the teaching of the most solemn and impressive personalities in the child's small world. The word "Jew" became a stimulus which touched off this emotion. It was aroused by every object and person to which the word was applied. It was a word to curse with.

I have written as if this were all in the past. But it is not. The pattern of the generic Christian response to the word "Jew" is in its essentials the same that it ever was. The teaching is in its essentials the same that it ever was. Anti-Semitism is an organic part of it. How much so, may be observed in those instances of young people who come from communities where there are no Jews but who have an extraordinarily passionate anti-Jewish complex. I have had numbers of such in my classes. I have seen them associate on terms of the warmest intimacy with fellow-students until the students were labeled for them, or labeled themselves, as Jews; and I have had occasion to observe the alteration of attitude which the application of that term to a personality evoked. I have discussed anti-Semitism with Christianized Chinese and Japanese who had never been exposed to the secondary, non-religious anti-Jewish prepossessions. The reaction seemed in all cases the unconscious response of a habit whose base was the religious preconception—the definition of the central rôle and status of the Jew in the Christian system.

Wherever this system is taught the preconception is transmitted. People are not conscious of it; it lies in the unconscious subsoil of their minds and gives tone and pattern to their contacts with Jews. Neither experience nor the liberalizing influences of the humaner disciplines, neither science nor higher criticism nor free society seem much to modify its influences. Even the liberal movements in the church itself are without much effect upon it. Rather do all these acquirements become grist for the mill and afford the original feeling new and more modern symbols of experience. In principle and practice the pseudo-science of the brilliant economist Sombart has no different drive from the mythologies of Henry Ford; the vaticinations of Renan and Gobineau have the same dynamics as the phobias of Daudet and Lothrop Stoddard; the hysterical anthropology of Houston Stewart Chamberlain is a rationalization of the same nature as the anthropological mythology of Madison Grant. In even so detached and contemplative a spirit as George Santayana the Sunday-school bogy rose, when Europe was shaken, as a body for the new fear, to explain and assuage it.

How many thousands of essentially free minds succumbed to it when inundated at the expense of Henry Ford with floods of anti-Semitic literature—forgeries so clumsy, inventions and lies so palpable that, with any other people as their theme, they would have been thrown into the waste-basket with a laugh! But because the Jews were their theme scores of friends and acquaintances of high intelligence, liberal spirit, radical interests and associations have asked me, troubled, whether there could really not be anything in it. Those to whose attention I called the underlying preconception which mothered the question, recognized it upon consideration, acknowledged it, and to that degree were freed of it. For most, it is not so easy. The thing lies too deep and too forgotten. Mr. Heywood Broun, therefore, seems too optimistic for the future of his son. The occasion which evoked his optimism is worth quoting at length, for it is an apt illustration of the point:

> H. 3d informed me that he couldn't play with Margaret any more. We didn't know who Margaret was, and yet the break seemed unfortunate. We asked him why he couldn't play with Margaret any more, and he said "because she is a Jew." Naturally that suggested another inquiry. "Because the Jews killed Christ," said H. 3d. No, at the present moment H. 3d is no more intelligent in his attitude toward race questions than the president of Harvard University, and he will be five on his next birthday. . . . Of course H. 3d is going to grow out of all that rubbish. He may pick up catchwords from Ku Kluxers, but after all he is a reasonable human being and we can argue with him and even spank him.

Attitudes that Sunday-schools the world over impart automatically to children at five may be deep buried and forgotten at five and fifty, but they are not extirpated, nor translated. They make a subsoil of preconceptions upon which other interests are nourished and from which they gather strength.

The insurgence of anti-Semitism at Harvard University, as everywhere, draws its energy from this subsoil. The case of Harvard is very richly in point, for in most of its features it is a reduplication—Harvardized—of the sordid class-conflict that prevails in the undergraduate society of most American institutions of learning and that goes on in the State institutions as the war of "Greek" and "barbarian." Its very interesting precipitation as a "Jewish question" gives it unique evidential point. Consider. The life of that academy, like the life of all the other endowed institutions of learning in the United States, goes on in two dimensions. One is ostensibly intellectual; the other is social. The first is organized about the classroom; the second is organized about the undergraduate club or fraternity. The classroom form is in the main a disagreeable price which those seeking the social cachet of being "college men" must pay for the privilege of participating in the clubroom form. Undergraduate feelings, interests, and ambitions are integrated by the latter; it sets the standards and establishes the patterns of undergraduate life. This is an antique arrangement maintaining itself victoriously against perennial challenge. The challenge is called democracy, but the necessary basis of democracy, particularly in the academic world, is social heterogeneity and intellectual diversification. Harvard, in the heyday of Eliot's presidency, had plausible claim to being such a democracy. It troubled his successor from the beginning, and the latter's whole policy has been aimed at the restoration of social homogeneity, of something akin to intellectual uniformity.

Harvard College was created to be a sectarian academy whose primary purpose was to breed Puritan preachers, and from the outset, through many generations, Harvard kept up a sectarian homogeneity of students and faculty. The inevitable processes of secularization, the demands of the new learning in science and in industry, diversified the faculty and dispersed it socially. With the student body, however, the new influences worked otherwise. The homogeneity of "Harvard families" was in no relevant sense broken up. The masses of newcomers became simply a heterogeneous aggregate of individuals among whom the aborigines maintained their associations in superior and unbreached detachment. Membership in the clubs was conditioned upon family relations, mitigated by wealth, school connection, and by athletic distinction. In this way the class conflict of the world outside reproduced itself in the college yard.

In recent years there have been added to the categories of this conflict—rich and poor, well-born and plebeian, gentlemen and grinds—another pair; native and foreign born. There has been a conspicuous increase in the number of foreign-born students, children of recent immigrants, in American colleges. Of these foreign-born students by far the larger number were Jews. The fact of their being Jews gave the conventional social issue its distinctive twist. Qualities characteristic of an economic grade could be referred to racial origins and sanctioned by the always active, if mostly unconscious, religious prejudice.

And so it was. While the Jews were few in number the discrimination against them was lost in the mass of class exclusions. As their numbers grew the discrimination grew, and grew in the degree that they developed to the full the traits of the most traditional and approved undergraduate social life—minus, of course, the Back Bay. They automatically submitted themselves to the completest assimilation possible, but they found that it takes two to effect an assimilation. Willing as they might be to fuse with the Christians, the Christians would not fuse with them. No clubs, no fraternities, few athletic teams, could find any place for them—with rare exceptions. Willy nilly, whether as amateur Gentiles or natural Jews, they were thrown back upon each other for the fellowship of college life. They created in their own circles what was refused them when they sought a wider one—the clubs, the fraternities, and such, which are the acme of undergraduate society, and they created them and lived and moved in them in the closest possible imitation of the prevailing approved and emulated traditional type.

Of course, the proper sort of undergraduate and professor—those who, in the language of the Hairy Ape, "belonged"—grew scared and disturbed. But for a long time nothing could be done—save by snobbery and innuendo —that would not lead to the public shame of an exposure of the effective overt motives in the anti-Jewish sentiment. After the armistice, action became easier and more plausible. The propaganda of czarist émigrés, the disseminations of Henry Ford, the association of Jews with "Reds," the resurgence of the Ku Klux Klan, the veiled though known and publicly discussed limitations upon Jews at Columbia, New York University, and other universities, provided a sympathetic social atmosphere and an encouraging academic precedent. Accusations of moral inferiority sprang automatically to the lips of their opponents and have not been withdrawn though proved to be false. Then the attack was shifted to the proposition that beyond a certain proportion—15 per cent, precisely—Jews are not assimilable. And so on. Anti-Semitic Europe— Hungary, Rumania, Germany, *et al.*, greeted these declarations with glee, and declared their own practices completely justified by them.

Of course the various rationalizations of his policy offered by Mr. Lowell and his defenders are excuses, not causes, in the case. For the fact is that it is not the failure of Jews to be assimilated into undergraduate society which troubles them. They do not want the Jews to be assimilated into undergraduate society. What really troubles them is the completeness with which the Jews want to be and have been assimilated. As every boy may yet be President, so, though perhaps with less certainty, every poor man's son might yet be a gentleman, and after a certain probation admitted to the society of gentlemen born. But if he is the son, not only of a poor man but of a poor man (or even of a rich) of the people who rejected the Savior and were thereupon rejected by God who sent the Savior, then his apparition—on his own—in gentleman's guise becomes a mockery, a vexation, and an irritant. Unaware of the unconscious roots in the emotions of ancestral religion men seek to justify this irritation and vexation by varied and contradictory rationalizations.

But here, as everywhere else, the root of the special Jewish difficulty is not racial, nor economic, nor caste. It does not arise in connection with any Christian stock involved—whether in America or in Europe—in similar racial or economic or caste differences. The root of the special Jewish difficulty is the teaching concerning the Jews integral to the scheme of salvation according to the Christian religion. When Christianity will effectively stop teaching that the Jews are enemies of God and of mankind it will strike anti-Semitism at its foundations.

1923

XIII

ON THE REVISION OF CHRISTIAN
TEACHING CONCERNING JEWS

During the ten years odd since I discussed in the public prints the sources of anti-Semitism, the emotional history of the Western world shows a widespreading upset, a deep spiritual unhealth. If religious change measures and expresses emotional disturbances, then the changing religious perspectives of Europe and America, to say nothing of the Asiatic countries, testify to an unprecedented depth in the post-war emotional disturbance. Whatever its causes may be—and the social-economic changes following the war are more than sufficient causes—its symptoms and its formulae find their easiest projections in the principles and postures of religion. These come as conscious voices of the unconscious malaise.

Respecting these, the role of the Jews remains, on the whole, traditional. In Europe it is still that of the devil of the piece. On the Jew are fathered all the evils which the post-war peoples of the continent suffer from. In the Jew, grafting and ambitious politicians, financiers and ecclesiastics continue to find at hand a scapegoat readymade by Christian history. Hitler or Cuza, Dmowski or Horthy—it does not matter what their principles are or their politics lead to, the major part is "Down with the Jews."

In the United States the situation is different. The war did not disorganize the national economy. It only heightened its tempo and led perhaps to the sharpening of the contrast between mania and depression, prosperity and unemployment, the peak and the trough of the business cycle. It hastened and intensified the crises which the industrialization of agriculture would have brought on anyhow, and it reinforced with the undischarged passions of the war-time the emotional disturbance natural to such crises.

The sentiments to which these conditions gave rise were of two kinds: one was internal to the Protestant world itself, the other was projected upon the outsider. Within the Protestant Church, issue was joined between Fundamentalism and Modernism. Evolution became a scapegoat for the dislocations brought on by the expansion of the factory system and the spread of machinery. There was a trial in which the two Americas, symbolized in Bryan and in Darrow, confronted each other, and Bryan died soon after. Outside of the churches, the role of scapegoat was distributed between the Negroes, the Roman Catholics and the Jews. By such organizations as the Ku Klux Klan, Protestantism was made a *sine qua non* of patriotism, and on the whole the Jews came off better in the propaganda of this organization than the Negroes or Catholics. It was the higher financial-social levels of the community that again laid the Jews upon the sacrificial altar in the traditional role of scapegoats.

This was in no small degree due to the influence of titled persons, army officers, and other ranks of emigré monarchists who had run away from the Russian revolution. These emigrés brought with them the historic anti-Semitism of their orthodox Christian inheritance. They infected with it professional sons and daughters of the American revolution, patrioteers concerned about big armies and navies, "society" leaders, and big-business men, the outstanding sample of the latter being the automobile-maker, Henry Ford. These social and vocational castes introduced, perhaps for the first time in American history, a type of anti-Semitism which antedates the Protestant reformation. They spread it thick and far as a conscious propaganda whose strength and range and influence the passing years have not diminished. This anti-Semitism is not of the masses, but of the classes. It infests the academic, professional, financial and technical worlds. It closes in on the Jews as a boycott from certain vocations and cuts down their participation in the spiritual life of the American people. Its implications for Americanism are as momentous as for the Jews, and no end is in sight. . . .

Against this unprecedented, counter-American development is to be set another movement. This movement is taking shape under the leaders of the Christian churches themselves. It is a social phenomenon for the moment difficult to evaluate. It cannot properly be called modernist, because the spokesmen for a great many fundamentalist churches share in it, yet it certainly looks back to nothing else than the development of the higher criticism and rests upon the implications of that for Christian teaching. In no small degree it appears to be a response to the secularizing pressure of science and industry upon ecclesiastical fortunes. The proselyting interest is a factor in it, and there are no doubt many other, equally potent, influences. Whatever they be, they are leading to a *rapprochement* of Christians with Jews. The decade has seen the making of several studies of the actualities of contact between Jews and Christians, one such being the work of the Inquiry into the Christian Way of Life. Good Will Committees and such like have held meetings and conducted conferences.

The high point of these eventuations came at Christmas, 1931. Then a Christmas Message was sent out to the

Christian world. Its subject was the relation between Christians and "our Jewish neighbors." Its signers were the heads of the leading Protestant church bodies of the United States and Canada, among them the Federal Council of the Churches of Christ of America, the Presbyterians, the Methodists, the Friends, the Lutherans, the Baptists, the Disciples, the Congregationalists, the Episcopalians, the Reformed Church, the Christian Associations, and the Home Missions and International Missionary Councils.

I subjoin the message:

At this season when the Christmas message of peace to men of good will is being sounded throughout the world, we Christians of the United States and Canada, mindful that this message was first proclaimed in the land of Israel to the Jewish people and that it has come to us through them, earnestly seek to emphasize its significance for us today; believing that the message from ancient Palestine, if truly accepted, can mellow and exalt all human relationships and hasten the time when men shall dwell together in peace.

We deplore the long record of wrongs from which the Jewish people have suffered in the past, often from the hands of those who have professed the Christian faith and who have yet been guilty of acts utterly alien to the Christian teaching and spirit.

We declare our disavowal of anti-Semitism in every form and our purpose to remove by every available means its causes and manifestations in order that we may share with our fellow citizens of Jewish heritage, every political, educational, commercial, social, and religious opportunity.

We urge upon Christians everywhere the cultivation of understanding, appreciation, and good will toward the Jewish people to whom we owe so much. We call upon all Christians as they commemorate the birth of Jesus at Christmas this year, to join us, through personal influence, the teaching of the young at home and school and in other ways, in earnestly seeking the removal of anti-Jewish prejudices and their consequences and the advent of a new era of friendly fellowship and cooperation worthy of the faith we profess.

No one can question the candor, the courage, and the magnanimity of this statement. Yet how can one not wonder if those who signed it realized, in the glow of generous emotion that impelled them to this action, all the implications of the pledge "to remove the causes of anti-Semitism by every available means," including the use of personal influence and the teaching of the young?

So deep and wide are the implications of these promises that I thought it just to call some of these to the attention of the signers. Accordingly, I wrote, in the columns of *Opinion* some comments on the Christmas Message, in the course of which I called attention to the significant revision of Christian teaching which it implies. Since that date some unexpected additional testimony regarding this teaching has come to hand from the pen of one of the princes of Imperial Russia, a near relative of the late Czar, the Grand Duke Alexander.

"It was not my fault," he writes in his recently published biography,* "that I hated the Jews, the Poles, the Swedes, the Germans, the British and the French. I blame the Greek Orthodox Church and the notorious doctrine of

---

* *Once a Grand Duke,* by The Grand Duke Alexander of Russia, Farrar and Rinehart.

official patriotism—beaten into me by twelve years of study—for my inability to treat with friendliness all these nations that had never committed a crime against me personally.

"Until I came into my first contact with the church, the word "Jew" signified for me an old smiling man who delivered chickens, turkeys, ducks and other poultry at our palace in Tiflis. I felt a genuine sympathy for the kind expression of his wrinkled bearded face, and could not believe that he traced his ancestry straight to Judas. But my reverend teacher persisted in his daily descriptions of the sufferings of Christ! He played on my childish imagination and succeeded in making me see a murderer and a torturer in every worshipper of Jehovah. My timid attempts at quoting the Sermon on the Mount were waved aside with impatience. "Yes, Christ did advise our loving our enemies," said Father Titoff, "but that should not affect our views of the Jews!" Poor Father Titoff! In his clumsy provincial way he was merely imitating the preaching of his betters who were promoting anti-Semitism for over eighteen centuries from the pulpits of the house of God. The Catholics, the Episcopalians, the Methodists, the Baptists, all these supposedly Christian creeds and denominations have equally contributed to the despicable cause of fostering hatred, while the anti-Jewish legislation of Russia found its principal support among the high priests of the Greek Orthodox Church. . . ."

One need not labor the point that this Christian teaching concerning the Jews is by no means confined to the clergy of the Orthodox Church; that, inevitably, this teaching is not sectarian but Christian as such.

It is this Christian teaching superimposed on the normal modes of negative contact through competition, conflict, opposition, dislike, which creates the difference between anti-Semitism and these other modes. The Germans may depreciate the French, the French the Russians, the Russians the English, the English the Americans, the Americans the Chinese, the Chinese the Japanese, the Japanese all occidentals, for good and sufficient cause. But that cause is not first and last the vile position which the people depreciated are assigned in the religious schemata of these several groups. Touching the relation of Christian society to the Jews, the reverse is the case. It is the religious teaching which constitutes the first difference and the last. It puts an acute accent on anti-Semitism. With respect to it, all other negative contacts and influences, reasonable or not, are of a secondary order. To alter them hence, to remove their causes, means first and foremost to remove the religious cause. And to remove the religious cause means to revise the attitude toward the Jews inculcated by the Christian scheme of salvation.

The editor of *Opinion* called the attention of the signers of the Christmas Message and of many other spokesmen for official Christendom to my comment on the Message. Such responses as were received fall broadly into two types. One of those may be called Modernist. It is summed up in the remarks of the Reverend Peter Ainslie of the Christian Temple in Baltimore. "The Christian attitude toward Jews," says Mr. Ainslie, "is based on a falsehood." Contrasted with Mr. Ainslie's comment is that of an editorial in the *Christian Examiner,* to the effect that: "any gesture of kindness by organized Christianity toward Judaism is declared by them to be a repudiation of Christian doctrine. . . . We insist . . . the Jews of the present day need to be saved by the blood of Jesus Christ." In the same logical line, but much less specific, is the commentary of the Reverend Dr. Knubel, President of the United Lutherans. Jesus being Jesus, (i.e., vicarious atonement for human sin) he must necessarily have been rejected by any and every people among whom he appears. "Consequently anti-Semitism in its common forms becomes clearly a vicious Phariseeism." Mr. Cogswell of the Missionary Education Movement, on the other hand, denies that Christian education in the United States carries any imputation against the Jews. Jesus' sufferings, he rationalizes, were simply a work "of evil men in a race that also had great and good men."

II

Save for Mr. Ainslie, the commentators miss the point involved. To him and his companions in the faith, the problem is simple and its solution a foregone conclusion. If I do not misinterpret them, the philosophy underlying his statement would be about as follows:

In our modern world of science and industry, the old supernaturalism of the Christian system is necessarily giving way before higher criticism, historical research, and the new sciences of nature and man. Jesus ceases to be the second person of the Trinity, incarnated on earth, crucified as a sacrifice for the sins of man, then returned to heaven to be again the second person of the Trinity. Jesus becomes an historic personage, a man among men, elected for reasons of tradition and history to be the pregnant symbol of ideals of civilized living among humane men and women of the Western world. The standard Christian theology gives way to a general philosophy of nature and man based on scientific knowledge and social goodwill. This philosophy provides a sort of natural and universal faith, the common denominator in all religious sects, not Christian only, but Mohammedan, Buddhist, Brahman, and Jewish as well. The sects do not lose their identity any more than different individuals who accept the multiplication table lose their individuality. The Presbyterians, the Baptists, the Episcopalians, the Judaists, they remain separate religious associations of people united by common traditions, common ways of life and worship and common emotions which go with those ways. The differences between sects are only so many particular and individual symbols, so many different metaphors for the same essential values which the mind discovers and the heart aspires to.

Such was the situation in the ancient world before Christianity took power. The sects of Dionysus, of Isis and Osiris, of Cybele, of Apollo, of Mithra, of Zeus, and of who knows how many other great gods, including Jehovah, lived together in amity as so many allegories, so many different poetic dramatizations of a common view of the nature and the destiny of man, which then went by the name of neo-Platonism.

This comity of cults, this freedom, tolerance and co-operation of religions, came to an end when Christianity was set up as the sole religion of the state, and Europe was launched upon a religious imperialism that lasted until the Protestant reformation. Today, science and industry are bringing back, slowly and with many reverses, but noticeably, here a little, there a little, something of the ancient comity. In America the pre-industrial founding fathers hoped to do this by means of the law of the land, a hundred and more years ago. The record shows how much or how little they succeed.

Your sect by sufferings (wrote Thomas Jefferson to Mordecai Noah), has furnished a remarkable proof of the universal spirit of religious intolerance inherent in every sect, disclaimed by all when feeble, and practiced by all when in power. Our laws have applied the only antidote to this vice, protecting our religious, as they do our civil rights, by putting all on an equal footing. But there remains much to be done, for although we are free by the law, we are not so in practice; public opinion erects itself into an Inquisition, and exercises its office with as much fanaticism as fans the flames of an *auto-da-fé*.

The prejudice still scowling on your section of our religion, although the elder one, cannot be unfelt by yourselves; it is to be hoped that individual dispositions will at length mold themselves to the model of the law, and consider the model basis, on which all religions rest, as the rallying point which unites them in a common interest. . . .

The Christmas Message is an indication that the Jeffersonian democratic hope has some ground in American social fact. During a score of years, and very noticeably during the last decade, the so varied sects have been coming closer together in practice as well as in sentiment. The endeavors of different doctrines and disciplines of the Protestant world to fuse both as worshipping congregations and as organized establishments provide telling evidence that among the leading Protestantisms of the United States differences have ceased to be so much more important than unity of interest. Even the orthodox Catholic bodies, Roman and not, have shown signs of a concern for reunion, although the papal notion of reunion consists in submission to, not equality with, Catholicism. But that the Protestant churches are being certainly and positively and hopefully vitalized by the modern point of view seems to me beyond question. One needs no more striking testimony than the spectacle of more advanced religious societies like Unitarian groups, or the Community Church, exchanging places of worship, ministers and services with establishments like the Free Synagogue and other religious societies of the Jews. Such events appear, moreover, to be taken as phases of living distinctions that nevertheless involve no vital differences.

III

With the Fundamentalists the situation remains still the one which Jefferson deplored. They necessarily rule out science and its implications. As Protestants they are ready to give unto Caesar what is Caesar's, but they cannot abate a jot or tittle of the supernatural scheme of salvation. Nor, for the purpose of revising the Jewish position in the Christian theological system, do they need to. It is only requisite that they should follow the logic of their scheme of salvation with singleness of mind and heart. For the standard teaching of Christianity about the Jew is no less obfuscated in logic and grim in feeling than ever.

If Jesus were accepted merely as a human being, and the crucifixion as a tragic episode in the political struggles of his time, the anti-Semitism implicated in Christian orthodoxy could be argued with some show of reason, even if without heart or wisdom. . . .

But to Fundamentalism Jesus is not a human being. To Fundamentalism Jesus is God himself as the second person of the Trinity. To Fundamentalism the crucifixion is not an unfortunate historic episode. To Fundamentalism the crucifixion is the central event in cosmic history, preordained by divine Providence as the expiation by God, in his role as the Son, of the sins of the world. . . . Without the crucifixion, the destiny of man is eternal damnation, not salvation. With it, the believer is redeemed forever.

This way of thinking about Jesus grew slowly into the form it received in the fourth Gospel. Its beginnings appear early in the history of the Christian communities.

They start in the legends of Jesus' resurrection and reappearance to his disciples. Not enough stress is laid on the fact that the first Christians were Jews, and that Christianity and the Christians were simply the teaching and communion of just another Jewish sect. As this sect grew in numbers and power, it also acquired invidious competitive interests. More and more it distinguished itself from Jewry and Judaism. The Christian sectaries, starting with Paul, developed first a non-Jewish, then anti-Jewish, Hellenistic salvation of their own. Where, in the early days, "salvation was of the Jews," it ceased to be so. In the course of time the anti-Jewish sentiment of the early Christians got elaborated into fixed theological rationalizations of the kind we are familiar with. The rationalizers identify the Jews as "deicides," Christ-killers. They regard them as cursed through the crucifixion, and they attribute to them any evil the world happens to be suffering from. They do not destroy them; they only subject them to torture and make them pay for the privilege. In the words of the Ecclesiastical Synod of 1542 in Poland: "The Church tolerates Jews for the sole purpose of reminding us of the torments of the Savior." Christian practice, especially intense from the time of the Crusades on, has been the exercise of a continuous revenge on the Jews for the Passion of Christ Jesus by the foreordained outpouring of whose blood the sins of man are washed away.

The irony of the record lies in the contradiction that it opposes to the supernatural premises on which Christian salvation is postulated. For the Christian treatment of the Jews implies that the Passion of the Lord was in fact not a cosmic climax predetermined by God's justice and mercy as a vicarious atonement for the sins of mankind. The Christian treatment of the Jews implies that Jesus was not

God but man. It implies that the crucifixion was not a divine atonement, but a human miscarriage of justice and act of injustice.

If Jesus was God and not man, if the crucifixion was atonement and not unmerited punishment, if the Passion was the high point in the divine scheme of saving the children of Adam from the consequences of Adam's sin, then all the agencies that were used to bring about the Passion were no less instruments in the salvation of mankind than the Savior himself. If Jesus is the Savior, the Jews are also saviors, since without them there would have been no Jesus and no vicarious atonement. Thus instead of obloquy for the reputed share in the crucifixion, they merit gratitude and honor. Their logical place in the Christian scheme of salvation is alongside that of Jesus, and not that of Satan. They deserve at least as much as Pilate to be regarded Christian saints.*

But the fact is that Christian doctrine has suffered since the beginning from a certain duplexity, and neither popes nor princes have taken seriously the crucifixion and its implications as a supernatural event. They used it simply as a ground for exploiting the helpless Jews in every possible way, and in a country like Russia continued to do so until the Revolution. In other parts of the world it was replaced by subtler and more refined methods and formulae, but it was not given up.

Those Christians who take the theological account of the crucifixion literally could abolish what is distinct in anti-Semitism, and bring into Christian thinking a rigorous and decent logic by thus assigning the Jews the status they logically merit in the scheme of salvation. The Christians would sacrifice nothing of their supernatural hope, and they would gain natural humanity and decency. For

* Pilate and his wife are worshipped as saints by the Abyssinian church.

those to whom the Passion of the Lord is a symbol, a poetic language, of the problem of each soul seeking its adjustment to a world which is not made for it, the candid treatment of the story *as* a symbol and a poetic language is all that is necessary. On the modernist side, Christianism is revising itself, and with it the position of the Jews in its theology. On the Fundamentalist side the revision can come only through a deliberate act. One expects nothing from the great monopolistic ecclesiastical establishments like the Greek or Roman Catholicisms, but among Protestant Fundamentalists, both social change and natural kindliness and intelligence would point to this consummation.

That it can take place is another story.

1932

XIV

"A CONTRADICTION IN TERMS"

"Modern students approach Judaism with prepossessions of so radically different an order that it requires an
effort of imagination to put ourselves at this point of view.
The idea of historical development in religion, as in science
and in institutions—in civilization as a whole—so dominates us that it is hard to understand a religion to which it
is a contradiction in terms. But it is idle to try to compre-
hend Judaism at all unless we are prepared to accept its
own assumptions as principles of interpretation, and not
substitute ours for them."

No, this paragraph is not by any mere "Jewish intellectual." It occurs in the recently published work on
Judaism * by one of the foremost biblical scholars of our
time and one of its most distinguished authorities on religions, the Frothingham Professor of the History of
Religions at Harvard University, George Foot Moore.

The work is in two monumental volumes and deals
with Judaism in the age of the Tannaim, that is, with
Judaism "in the centuries in which it assumed definitive
form, as it presents itself in the tradition which it has
always regarded as authentic." These volumes offer, I
believe, the only definitive exposition by a modern scholar
of the Judaism that, until the middle of the nineteenth
century, was the definitive faith of "Catholic Israel." The

* *Judaism in the First Centuries of the Christian Era.* Vol. I, p. 112.
Harvard University Press.

first study of the kind in the English language, it seems indubitably destined to be the classic of this domain of scholarship.

Professor Moore is not only a prince of modern scientific method in the study of religions; he is also not a Jew, and not a Judaist. He approaches his materials and sources from a background of knowledge of other religions as well as Judaism whose range and scope are unique among higher critics, he handles them with a sureness which derives from the intimacy of thirty years' study, and with a sympathetic impartiality which springs not merely out of the richness and depth of his scientific information, but out of a freedom from those almost inevitable prejudices of controversy and allegiance to which a Jewish writer could at the very best not attain. If Professor Moore's work deals with controversy or prejudice at all, it glances in the direction of such distortions as appear in the proverbial judgments regarding the "scribes and Pharisees," "legalism," and the like. The record is brought to bear on the distortions and automatically they are corrected. So successfully has Professor Moore put himself at the point of view of the "radically different order" which Judaism historically is, that the work might be attributed to some ideally-equipped orthodox rabbi, creating a new compendium of the faith for a faithless world.

Yet this success has its disadvantages. With all its otherness, as a "radically different order," Judaism was still the faith that living men and women actually lived by, more or less, and its rules and verbal categories and formulae, however sacred, could hardly be anything more than instruments and symbols in the enterprise of life. What essentially Professor Moore's work provides is an anatomy—and at that a descriptive rather than an analytical anatomy—of Judaism. It enables you to realize Judaism as a structure more than as a living national institution with a history and problems. The historic process of the group life comes to you as suggestion and inference, not as demonstration, and it comes from the rich citation of which much of the work consists. Against the inert background of the lucid anatomical context, this brings you a sense of the permanent peculiarity of the case of Judaism, that core of practices and professions which has remained "the same" from the age of the Tannaim to the present day, and which stays still the religion of the great majority of the Jews who remain Judaists.

What you find in these practices and professions immediately leads you to wonder. It leads you to wonder about exactly those matters of historical development which Professor Moore excludes. It moves you to speculate, first, upon the causes that created Judaism and, second, upon the causes that sustained it. It leads you to wonder about these things, that is, if you are at all disturbed by the present position of the Jews, and of Hebraism and Judaism, and are concerned about their future.

For the present is critical and the future is dubious, and only an appreciation and control of causes as the scientist is supposed to appreciate and control causes is able to resolve the one and assure the other. Such an attitude towards causes seems so far to have been impossible among Jews who are first Judaists, especially among those officially responsible for the maintenance and perpetuation of Judaism. It is not without significance that the greatest "higher critics" have not been Jews, and that the best work upon Judaism has been written by a non-Jew. Least of all can it be without significance that the unquestionable authority of this scholar implies that the modern point of view and historical Judaism stand in such contradiction to one another that without falsification of its peculiar nature Judaism cannot be thought in modern terms at all.

Professor Moore's work brings out more clearly than ever that the peculiar nature of Judaism does not lie in the Judaistic "idea" of God. Properly speaking, indeed, there cannot be said to have been a Judaistic idea of God in the sense in which there have been Greek or Christian ideas of God. Ideas of God are items in philosophical discourse. They are made and perfected by ratiocination and dialectic; they involve the systematic use of reason and emerge in a theology. But in Judaism, as Professor Moore points out, such matters are conspicuous by their absence.

Nor does the peculiarity of Judaism lie in its ethical ideas. Professor Moore's work makes the observation more clearly and certainly than ever that Judaism did not have a system of ethics; "the Jews did not develop ethics as a branch of philosophy, a science of conduct and character, such as we have in mind when we speak of the ethics of the Greeks. . . . What are called Jewish ethics are in substance and form described as preceptive morals . . . no attempt is made to systematize these precepts . . . such virtues as filial piety, philanthropy or charity have no measure or norm, but are left to the conscience and right feeling of the individual, *masur la-lev,* committed to the heart." In a word, the phrase "ethical monotheism" is a schismatic phrase; it represents what historically Judaism is not; it does not represent what Judaism historically is.

Not even the nationalism of the religion, nor its peculiar doctrine of "the life to come," nor any of what might be called its theological implications truly set forth its dynamic essence.

This dynamic essence is to be found in the peculiar ways of behaving that being a Judaist imposes on a man; that is, in the *observances* of Judaism. The character and survival-power of Judaism reside in these observances. Doctrines and ideas are in fact functions derived from these observances and dependent on them. Reform, which begins as a dropping of observances, terminates as a transformation of doctrines and ideas.

The observances of which Judaism is essentially made up are all equally obligatory. They are not divided or classified by the rabbinical experts. The obligation is the same whether for folkways, ceremonials or morals. It is imposed by the authority of the God of the Jews. It is imposed through the Torah or Law of the God. This law is a *revelation* vouchsafed, through the prophet Moses, in the Pentateuch and elaborated and expounded by the subsequent prophets, the scribes and the rabbis. It is a twofold law, written and oral, and equally compulsive in both aspects. It is a *revealed law,* and religion consists in obedience to it: "The whole of religion was revealed— nothing was kept back in heaven—and the whole content of revelation was religion." History, the record of the people, could neither impair nor improve this religion. Perfect it came from the mouth of God; perfect it remains in relation to Jews. They may come and go, be righteous or wicked, sinful or repentant, winners of a share in the life to come or not; but the Torah goes on forever, unaltered and unalterable, and alone to be followed and obeyed for forgiveness and salvation.

Two qualities especially signalize the revealed Law. One is its immutability. The other is its statutory char-

acter. Torah is "statute of the King of Kings," commandment that nothing can change. It is the order issued
once and for all by a ruler who rewards obedience with
life and fortune here or happiness in the "life to come"
and who punishes disobedience even unto the fourth
generation. As such, it is infallible. There can be no evasion of what it enjoins; performance is inevitable in all
times and all places. Failure to hear and to obey is sin,
which yet may be wiped out by repentance and be for-
given.

But, though infallible and unchanging itself, the Torah
nevertheless must be applied day by day in a world all
change, by men all fallibility. Its relation to man and the
world is thus in no sense of the type envisaged in science
or philosophy. It is neither a distillation of their essences
nor a vision of their characters. Rather is it like an order
issued by a general for the conduct, not of a battle, but
of a war. Not for nothing is the Word of the Lord described as the "Yoke of the Law." Judaists are harnessed
up in it, and made to go upon a way they would not and
do not spontaneously seek.

The adjustment of immutable statutes to a changing
world presented a problem which the makers of Judaism
solved as this problem is solved wherever a written, therefore a fixed, rule is applied to an undetermined existence.
Every word, every letter of the rule becomes supremely
important, for into words and letters must be injected
the various and conflicting meanings that a chanceful life
requires, and what is injected must seem to be derived.
Hence, if everlasting revelation is to be rendered relevant
to passing present needs, the method of interpretation
becomes of supreme importance: there develops "an
atomistic exegesis, particularly in juristic deductions and
inferences." By means of them the living, operative be-

ing of what Professor Moore so aptly calls "normative Judaism" is constituted and is enabled to carry on.

Read "legalism" for "normative Judaism," and you will have the derogatory way of characterizing the national religion of the Jews. Once, however, you understand the premises and method of Judaism, you see that the legalism of the Judaists is no different in nature from the legalism of any other people, insofar as their lives are governed by law and by precedent deriving from that law. Such legalism is spontaneous and inevitable. It occurs everywhere, because everywhere men, feeling themselves at the mercy of change and chance, find it necessary to imagine some unchanging and infallible Law or Ideal to which they can cling and by which they can live.

What difference exists between the Law which the Jews idolized and the laws that other peoples worshipped for salvation is difference in attributive source and scope. Torah is attributed to the will of Jehovah; is the revelation of that will. Its scope is coincident with the entire enterprise of living.

Such an enterprise, as everybody feels and nearly everybody refuses to see, will be anything but logical. Neither, hence, can the application of law to it be logical. It must be all compromise, adjustment, reconciliation of contradictory and, from the point of view of pure reason, ultimately irreconcilable elements. It cannot move from universal premise to particular conclusion; it cannot consist of syllogistic reasoning; it can only go from precedent to precedent and justify one way of behaving that seems, at the time, in the place and under the circumstances good and desirable, by rules and precedents drawn from other times and circumstances and places. It can create custom, not principle. Its work is to establish, within the given limits of conduct and thought, reasonableness, not reason. Reasonableness is arbitral; it enables conflicting elements to live together without destroying one another. Reason is absolute; it must exclude and reject; it imposes the deductive oneness of dialectical consistency.

In "normative Judaism," hence, practice is far more important than profession. The Judaist is identified by what he does or refrains from doing, far more than by what he believes or does not believe. Judaism, he declares, is a religion of observances, not doctrines. In this used to lie its strength. For more than six centuries there "was nothing that deserves the name of schism"; and for that matter, there was hardly anything after, till the rise of the Reform movement in the nineteenth century. The reason? Professor Moore's own words state it best: "The ground of this remarkable unity is to be found not so much in a general agreement in fundamental ideas as in a community of observance throughout the whole Jewish world. Wherever a Jew went he found the same system of domestic observance in effect. This was of especial importance in the sphere of what are now called the dietary laws. . . . If he entered the synagogue he found everywhere the same form of service with minor variations. . . . Hebrew seems to have been generally used. . . ."

The dogmas and doctrines of Judaism, its "fundamental principles," differed from systematic theology or philosophy deriving from other religions in that they never attained an independent existence, but remained always attached to observances as rules or rationalizations for them.

As ideas these dogmas and doctrines unmistakably reveal this connection. If you compare the idea of the Jewish God as he is elicited by the rabbis from Torah and tradition with the unlegalistic, logically-conceived gods of the philosophers and the theologians of whatever times, you will find that the Jewish God is an idea made up of irreconcilable elements, and that these elements are untranslated symbols of the experiences of Jewish life, selected by interest and tradition: Jehovah appears as a personality, yet without personal characteristics; imageless, yet maker of man in his image; near and remote in the world, yet out of it; just, yet merciful; the source of both good and evil fortunes, omnipotent, yet face to face with a world in which man at least is free; omniscient, yet forgiving sin to the truly repentant. The qualities of Jehovah and of the total experience of a community transmitted in rules by memory and tradition are here interchangeable. Pragmatically the one turns out to be only a verbal precipitation from the other.

Now such experiences and their precipitation, to be repeated and believed, must be preserved in memory and transmitted in habit. To a great degree they are accidental, and that which makes up their individuality is only contingent in the nature of things; that is, it got started by accident and is kept going by struggle; it didn't have to happen or to survive. Professor Moore's observation that in Judaism basic human relations are "without measure or norm . . . and left to the conscience and right feeling of the individual," while the residue of religion is subject, often, to the utmost refinement of juristic casuistry, is here conclusive. This difference in treatment between morals and ceremonial comes from the fact that morals, being implicit in the very nature of the common life, renew themselves automatically if on occasion they lapse. Ceremonials, on the other hand, are artifacts, and unless artificially preserved and transmitted, are destined to change and ultimately to disappear. For their survival and prosperity they require other aid than their own force and virtue.*

This aid can be supplied only by education. The happy fortune which established the synagogue as an institution of the Jewish community, with its accessory the school, saved the Judaism we know from the attrition and, at last, the extinction that overtook its competitors and rivals. Begun perhaps as a surrogate for worship in the temple among Jews who for one reason or another could not worship there, the synagogue won in the course of time a status of its own as a place where public worship consisted largely in learning and teaching the Law, not in sacrifice and offering; where the rabbi was more important than the priest and the word became as significant as the act.

> The consequence [writes Professor Moore] of the establishment of such a national worship for the whole subsequent history of Judaism was immeasurable. Its persistent character and, it is not too much to say, the very preservation of its existence through all the vicissitudes of its fortunes, it owes more than anything else to the synagogue. . . . Men of insight must have learned from the apostasy of many in high places [during the Maccabean struggle] and the indifference of the most that there was nothing more urgent to do than to inculcate and confirm religious loyalty by worship, knowledge, and habit, through some such means as the synagogue. The permanent security of the religion, to say nothing of the greater things it held in prospect, could only be attained by

* For a fuller analysis of this point, see my *Why Religion*, Chapter XIX, Section 9.

bringing all classes to an understanding of the distinctive nature of Judaism, an appreciation of its incomparable worth, and a devotion to its peculiar observances like that which the Pharisees themselves cultivated in their pledge-bound societies. Education in revealed religion which has its revelation in sacred scriptures is of necessity education in the Scripture; methodical instruction in the law was, under these conditions, the foundation of everything. Hence the regular readings from the Pentateuch, accompanied by an interpretative translation into the vernacular and followed by an expository or edifying discourse, usually taking something in the lesson as a point of departure, became constant elements of the synagogue service.

The synagogue implied the school, for its worship could not be carried on by the illiterate. Hence, "in some form or other the school is as old as the synagogue if not older, and the synagogue was always dependent upon it. . . . The obligation to maintain schools is repeatedly emphasized. . . . The endeavor to educate the whole people in its religion created a unique system of universal education, whose very elements comprised not only reading and writing, but an ancient language and its classic literature. The high intellectual and religious value thus set on education was indelibly impressed on the mind and one may say on the character of the Jew, and the institutions created for it have perpetuated themselves to the present day." Study of the Law came to be regarded as a necessary part of piety, an equivalent of all the supreme virtues, a service of the Lord in worship, like prayer. The high regard in which Jews held the student of the Law is proverbial, and this status passes over today to students in secular disciplines.

Now Judaism had its rivals and competitors in antiquity both within and without the Congregation of Israel. However these may be envisaged, they were of its moral and intellectual kin. They did not, even in their most rationalist and atheistic forms, stand to it in a relationship of fundamental contradiction. Whether as Platonism, or Stoicism, or Epicureanism, or Christianism, or any of the religions of antiquity, they rested on presumptive immutable principles as definitely given once and for all as the Torah itself, and in practice they solved the problem of accommodating principle to particular in much the same way. The "idea of historical development" was as foreign to them as it was to Judaism and instruction of the masses was an unheard-of idea. Instruction through the school and the synagogue gave Judaism a tremendous advantage over its competitors and they lapsed while it survived.

In the course of the last hundred years, however, new rivals have become effectively competitive. There has occurred a radical transformation in the basic intellectual atmosphere. Revealed religions find themselves in a progressively alien world to which they are a contradiction in terms. In this world, education is not the exception but the rule; *cheder* and Talmud Torah and *yeshivah* are confronted by universal and compulsory systems of public education, from kindergarten to college. The Judaist observances requiring a difficult self-denial and self-discipline are confronted with less exacting ways of life, for which the sanction is equal; the lore of the synagogue must meet in rivalry the lore of the laboratory and the field. Schools are empty, synagogues are empty; "normative Judaism" is being worn down as once it wore down Sadducee and Essene and Christian and Hellenist. What must it do to be saved in a world to whose spirit it is "a contradiction in terms"?

Professor Moore's great book is naturally not designed to provide an answer to this problem. But in showing what Judaism is, it throws an amazing light on the nature of the problem and on its conditions; it sharpens its outlines and points its position. It enables those Jews who are concerned in keeping the varied aspects of the Jewish spirit alive and operative in the complex manifold of a civilization grown inwardly alien to see more clearly what their task is and to consider more relevantly what they must do. If it shows Judaism at bay in a world to which its formulations are a contradiction in terms, it also indicates what means its own nature possesses to make peace with this world and grow there with new life and strength. Some of these means I have sketched in other essays of this book. Some are to be elicited only by the process of struggle itself. All perforce must involve techniques which will transform contradiction into consistency, conflict into growth.

1928

XV

CAN JUDAISM SURVIVE IN THE UNITED STATES?

It was on the train to Chicago. He was one of those young men who attract attention by their clothes. Not because his were loud or otherwise in poor taste. Rather because they were in too good taste. His style, like that of some kinds of writing, was too meticulous not to call attention to itself. It did not quite allow the personality to shine through; it seemed not altogether a part of him, not altogether to be taken for granted. I have noticed that many admirable young Jews dress like that. Whether this young man was a Jew not even the most sensitive and expert taste in Nordics could determine. He was tall, he was slim, his hair was very blonde, his eyes were very blue. There seemed to be a suggestion of Jew in the feel of him—something in his expression.

He passed my compartment twice within fifteen minutes, each time with the manner of one wanting to speak. The third time he stopped, and ventured my name. I nodded.

"Thought I recognized you. You won't remember me? Jonah Gutman? I used to be in your 'Theories of Life' class in Wisconsin."

I did remember him, and asked him to sit and chat. He had been a graduate student, had come up from one of the eastern colleges, looking for academic democracy and a higher degree in political economy. I remembered

him as being much stirred up about "the Jewish problem";
he came several times to talk with me about it. He was
one of those rare youngsters who took the dogma of the
"mission of Israel" seriously—the rabbi in whose Sunday-
school class he had acquired it seems to have been an
imposing personality, with power to influence adolescents mystically—and at college the lad had been a leader
in providing high-sounding ideals for his fraternity and
creating a student congregation. He had even dabbled
with Menorah affairs and attended meetings of undergraduate Zionists, but couldn't quite stomach that crowd.
None of these Jewish "activities" had satisfied. The Jewish fellows seemed somehow off; their high vocation as
scions of a priest-people seemed to coincide with conduct
and manners in no way better than they should be; those
of his own economic class were vulgar; so many of the
Zionists and Menorahites seemed to him foreign and
queer. His spirit was most at home with certain Christians
who shared his tastes and understood his problems. Almost he was on the point of that inwardness of friend-
ship with one of them which justifies the residual futility
of college life, but it did not quite come off. He was
stranded, alone, between the Jews he could not warm to
and the Christians who could not warm to him. His mind
was turned from the immediacies of religious emotion and
the Jewish problem to the—he imagined—less personal
ardors of social reconstruction and world peace. When he
was graduated he went West, ill at ease. He fared there
no better than in the East. The Judaist dogma, he felt,
lacked content; it now seemed to him irrelevant to the
things that mattered in the modern world. But the propaganda of peace and social justice seemed almost as little
disciplined to reality. By what ideal could a man honestly
live, seeing the chasm that opened always instantly be-

tween ideals and events? This was the perplexity he brought to me. But we had little talk on it. Before he had been six months in Madison his father died; he had had to go home to a considerable Pennsylvania city to take charge of the business. That was ten years ago. The business had prospered in his charge. He was now a very solid and respected member of his community, a husband, and father of three children. He showed me their pictures.

And yet—the emotional undertone which was apparent in the disharmony between his dress and person was apparent also in his success as an American. It was the same thing that one felt about him in his school days; unconscious now, but very much there, and near enough to the waking surface of his life to be animated by the old associations I represented. He broke at once into the old philosophy, and you could see that it was the deeply inward insecurity that drove him. What was it all about? he demanded. What were the values of his successful life? He did what his neighbors did and lived as they lived. He was a member of all the clubs and contributed to all the charities; he had a welfare department in his factory, and if weren't for the Chamber of Commerce would have an agreement with the Union. He underwrote the orchestra and held shares in the Little Theatre company. He was chairman of the Civic Reform Committee and on the board of directors of the Saturday Lunch Club. He was one of the governors of the Brookside Country Club— the only Jew in the club, he said in a tone whose bitterness was not without pride, and one of the Executive Committee of the Y. W. C. A. drive. And, of course, he was in Jewish affairs: that is, he paid what they asked and sat on committees when he couldn't get out of it. And a member of the Temple, to be sure. No, he didn't go much. He was as little at ease there as in the country club. Sermons bored him, and the rabbi seemed a dilettante, without much mind or backbone. He followed whatever fashions were current. Most rabbis did, he noticed, but he didn't hold it against them; they had to, to hold their jobs, which seemed to consist mostly in keeping the members of the congregation in good conceit with themselves and perpetuating the mission of Israel through talks to kids in Sunday schools. Spiritual leaders? Hardly. Poor guys making a better living than their fathers did. He didn't begrudge them that, but why the religious talk and highfalutin pretense?

Yes, his own children went to Sunday school—the two older ones. He didn't know why he sent them—both he and Mrs. Gutman were really agnostic—just not to make talk, he guessed. And it was funny to hear the youngest read the *Kiddush* from the English card on such Friday nights as there was family dinner. No, his social relations with Christians were purely formal. He and his wife played with Jews pretty exclusively. Always had, come to think of it; seemed the natural, the inevitable thing. Why? he wondered. Modern Americans have about the same religion, whoever their fathers were; they certainly live in the same way and conform to the same standards. Yet the intimacies of Jews are with Jews and of Christians with Christians. Of course, there was this new curse of anti-Semitism in the country, the Klan, and all that; but that only brought into notice what had always been so. . . .

He left me without the consolation his confession should have won him. I had none to give. Poor Jonah! entangled in the network of the crossing strands of American life like a honey bee in a spider's web. The best of the type of prosperous native Jew! What portent was he, I found myself asking, for the future of Judaism in the United States? For the future of the Jews?

II

It is the reflections which this question started off that I am setting down here. They do not pretend to be either prediction or prophecy. They do not pretend to be more than rather superficial speculations on the current trends of the national life and their bearing on the prospects of the Jewish communities and the Jewish religion that are a part of it. What, I thought, are its underlying dynamic units? What are their character, force and direction?

Ruminating over the data in which answers to these questions are to be sought, I found myself immediately confronted with an obstruction. The obstruction is that aggregate of prejudice and ideology with which both Jews and Christians have clothed the body of Jewry, particularly Christians. These are as a concealing garment that must be stripped away. It is the bare facts that call to be inspected, and the bare facts are what a visitor from, say, China would see whose mind had never been influenced by peculiarities of Jewish theology and Christian dogma; who had never been infected by anti-Semitic anthropology or its Jewish refutations; who had never heard anti-Semitic social history or its Jewish alternates.

The bare facts are what would emerge from the use of scientific method over a long period in the study of the origin, structure and activities of the Jewish communities in the American social environment; of the interaction between them; of the transformations it brings about in the groups, the institutions and the individuals who together compose the society of Jews in the United States.

Such a study does not exist. Such facts are not known.

The need to know them is barely felt by American Jews. At present they are content with a body of ideas about American Jewry which belongs to the categories of fantasy. The origins of these ideas do not lie in observation. The origins of these ideas lie in tradition. Their data are not sought in experience. Their data are accepted from books and sermons. Their energies are not those seen to be inherent in the community, its institutions and its members. Their energies are the blind emotions generated by the impact of the American scene upon traditional doctrines and practices. They, the ideas, are the projections and precipitates of the emotions; a pattern or figure of the collective Jewish personality, serving in part as a discharge of the feelings which generate it, and in part as an evasion of the harsh conjunctions with reality which engender and sustain the feelings.

The outlines of this personality-image of the Jewish people are familiar: a nation especially chosen by Jehovah to worship him; to testify that he is the only one of his kind; either concentrated in Palestine or scattered among the nations of the earth, a priest-people with the mission of vindicating and preaching "ethical monotheism."

The existence, the functions and the causes of this personality-image of the Jewish people would be one item in the manifold of items that make up the actual Jewish group-personality whose total behavior in the American scene a free and scientific observer would study.

III

When compared with the multiplicity and variety of the traits that enter into the pattern of Jewishness, the traditional personality-image appears as exceedingly abstract and simple. Professional Jews deal with this image as if it were a self-sufficing and invariant essence that persists and acts in the same way in every environment. The pulpit, indeed, treats it as if it had no environment, as if it endures *saecula saeculorum* unchanged in the void. But this is purely a convention of the cloth. Actually, the environment is a transforming influence, natural and social, beyond estimation; in point of fact there never exists an item that is just Jew or Judaism or Jewishness; it is always in addition Russian or American or German or Palestinian. And the adjectival factors so penetrate the substantive ones that in considerable proportions it is they that become substantive and the Jew adjectival. This is why it is of the first importance to get some insight into the dominant trends of the American scene and how they enter into and transform the constitutions of the Jewish communities that live and move and have their being among them.

Of these trends, the first and most general is religion. It is also the most ancient and perhaps the most important. I have shown * in another essay how "the Jewish problem" is automatically created by the position assigned the Jews in the Christian scheme of salvation. In this scheme, the Jews are a people chosen by God who have become a people rejected by God and who are thus by theological predestination outlaws from the fellowship of mankind; inherently inferior; inadmissible to the tasks and privileges of equals in the secular no less than the religious enterprises of the common life. There is no mode of anti-Semitism which does not take its departure from this presumption: sects of political economy, anthropology and history are founded on extensions of it to those disciplines. The ways that it has entered into the psyche of the Jews are subtle and numberless; nearly all the observable qualities invoked empirically to justify anti-Jewish

* "The Roots of Anti-Semitism."

prejudice are traceable to it. And it is, of course, the source of the actual disabilities under which Jews have lived and labored from the beginnings of imperial Christianity to the French Revolution, from the French Revolution to the present day.

How these actual disabilities have reacted on the Jewish psyche is notorious. For one thing they had to be accepted, as the conditions of any life whatsoever in the Christian environment; and accepting them meant incorporating them into Jewish habit, so that they became conditioning overtones in the Jewish way of life. But precisely because they were disabilities, they could not be so incorporated without conflict. The repressions they established in fact were automatically compensated for in idea: inferiorities now felt and suffered were nullified by the fantasy of superiorities unseen but to be revealed in the future. More than ever did the Jews fancy themselves as the Chosen People, the darlings of Jehovah, predestined to an ultimate visible supremacy among the families of mankind. The group-reaction to this inferiority of status was registered among its members as that combination of servility and aggression which critics of Jews often signalize as an inborn trait, together with a whole combination of other qualities that disappear wherever the habits and feelings of inferiority have been worn down enough to allow original impulses to flow naturally and freely. So far as I have been able to observe, however, the latter state has been attained only in sporadic and unrepresentative instances. To what degree inferiority of status and the feelings correlative still prevail may be measured by the emphasis laid on the compensatory doctrines of the "mission of Israel" and the "chosen people."

IV

Against the influence of the religion of the western world may be set the action of all those agencies and institutions usually called "modern." Outstanding among them are science, industry, political democracy, the public school systems. They affect Christianity no less than they affect Jews and Judaism, and in so far forth they mitigate, though they cannot nullify, the power of the religious tradition. The religious tradition is what gives the Christian response to Jewry its primary emotional tone; sets attitudes; determines valuations; so that even the sciences of man and nature may show a Christian disposition, and psychology and history and economics be so formulated as to justify views men have become ashamed to hold in the name of religion. On the whole, however, modern institutions of intellect and action tend to be equalizers.

Now the direction which equalization takes is naturally "upward." The social processes in which it is accomplished are imitative, and social imitation, when other things are equal, is an imitation of that which is *felt* to be superior. Thus, the social, religious and intellectual movement of Jewry is toward sameness with Christians; Jews throw off what is peculiar to themselves and take on what is characteristic of their superiors. Had Jewry not felt inferior, the emancipation of the Jews which began early in the 19th century would have resulted in the transfusion into the veins of Jewish group-life of the achievements and trends of modernity; would have resulted in their Hebraization. The actual story of the emancipation is the story of the progressive attrition of Jewish individuality, the dilution instead of the enrichment of the flavor of Jewish difference, the de-Judaization of the Jew to the pattern presented by my young friend Jonah Gutman.

Of course, the process has not been equally rapid for all levels of income, that is, all classes of Jews, nor the same for all European enclaves. The Jews of the United States are divided into orders and castes whose character cannot be described in simple terms. Moreover, they are in considerable economic and social flux; their boundaries are indeterminate and overlap; their centers are losing solidity and changing form and structure. As a totality, they do not present the picture of an integrated social group conscious of its corporate personality, alive with a common purpose and working out, by means of the compenetration of its inheritance and its environment, the social patterns and spiritual significances of an organized common life at once Jewish and American. Although efforts at integration, even intense and passionate efforts, are discernible in this American aggregation of Jewries, they do not seem to be efficacious; the cohesion of the parts is due far more to the inertia of tradition and the pressure of fear than to the inward propulsion of common interests and common ideals fulfilling themselves in common institutions. The parts intermingle, but there is no common center of Jewish nature about which they can group themselves, no common direction of Jewish tracing in which they can move.

For numbers, vitality and corporate Jewishness, easily the first of these parts is the body of poor industrial workers who inhabit the Bronx and the lower East Side of New York, the West and Northwest sides of Chicago, and have their well-defined quarters in every large city of the land. In the lives of these Judaism tends to be no more than a survival worn down to certain dietary intolerances, an occasional *kaddish* for the dead, and perhaps a ticket admitting to synagogue or hall on Rosh Hashanah and Yom

Kippur. They are not members of synagogues. They have no interests in the transmission of Judaism to their children. They do not care about Hebrew. Their free energies —those not taken up by the day's work—are absorbed in the politics of their unions and of the socialist parties. Their spiritual pabulum is a mixture of the unconscious tradition, the "radical" Yiddish press, the Yiddish theatre, and the standard-making uniformities of Americanism— newspaper boiler-plate, picture-palace films. Yiddish, a Yiddish as American as Pennsylvania Dutch, is their medium for the intimacies of social communication and cultural expression, the channel of their emotional life and their free interests. In so far as they are conscious of a social inheritance and a cultural tradition at all, and desirous to transmit and to develop it, it is this secular inheritance and tradition they appreciate and seek to pass on. They are the majority of the Jews in the land; if Judaism has a future with them, it is not discernible in their present attitude and interests.

The next group in the order of significance might roughly be described as the Jewry of the lower middle and middle classes. Very roughly. For this group is most solidary in the character of its vocation rather than its income level. That is exceedingly variable; Jews who by their incomes may belong to the great bourgeoisie are, because of their habits of life, mental attitude and dominant interests, members of this class. It is composed mostly of the shopkeepers, the tradesmen, the contracting employers, the white-collar proletarians, the small manufacturers, the bankers, the schoolmasters, and so on. Their characteristic income level is doubtfully higher than that of the organized factory-employees. They are distinguished from the latter mostly in being their own men; making a living has for them the insecurity of a specula-

tion and an adventure. Mostly of the recent migration,
they carry with them lively recollections of such education in Judaism as they had received. The insecurity of
their livelihoods is personal; it keeps awake in them the
sense of risk and of the importance of fortune; it renders
the grace of God a matter of import in the daily grind.
Accordingly, Judaism signifies to this class values the industrial workers are under no necessity to regard. And
accordingly it is this class who compose the bulk of the
membership of the orthodox synagogues of the land, recruit-
ing such societies as the Congregation of the Men of
Kalvaria or Shnipishok or Bolotke. It is their sons who
are sent to the *cheders* and *talmud torahs* and in their due
proportions graduated into the conservative and reform
theological seminaries. It is they who are prevailingly the
members of the Zionist organization, the supporters of
the Hebrew press, and the transmitters of the neo-Hebrew
culture. Their vernacular also is Yiddish, but they read
the *Tog* or *Tageblatt,* not the *Vorwärts.*

From their ranks, largely, emerge the various types of
clothing manufacturers, the bankers, the cotton factors,
the commission merchants, the lawyers, physicians, "realtors," building contractors and construction engineers
who live on a superior income level but retain the habits
of life and ways of thought of their poverty and struggle.
These are the patrons and benefactors of such undertakings
to harmonize traditional Judaism with the currents and
institutions of modern life as are to be seen in the Miz-
rachi, in the endeavor after the establishment and maintenance of Jewish parochial schools, in the project for a
new "modern" Yeshivah, and conspicuously in that imaginative adventure in harmonization, the Society for the
Advancement of Judaism, captained by Rabbi M. M.
Kaplan. Some of this class are drawn into the byway of

"Jewish Science," that interesting appropriation of the dogmas of Christian Science by the adjective Jewish. Negligible in number are the children of this class who are touched by the tradition their fathers pay to carry on, and who take the torch from their fathers' hands. Their number grows, if anything, smaller.

So, in spite of these efforts to integrate them, the fissure between the tradition of Judaism and modernity communicated by the public schools, the public prints and the public *mores* seems to widen rather than to narrow; they live together only where one or both are inert. Judaism, like Christianity, is not successfully competing with its secular rivals. The young don't care about Judaism.

That the young don't care about Judaism is even truer of the children of the prosperous Jews of native and west European origin. The total membership of the reform congregations numbers no more than 50,000. It now hardly ever sends one of its sons into the rabbinate. Its children graduate from the Sunday school into an indifference to Judaism which anti-Semitic revivals or untoward personal experiences may shock into a reblazoning of the compensating dogma of "the mission of Israel" or into an uneasiness about this irrelevant and troublesome burden of being a Jew. Being a Jew, for any member of this group, is in fact only remotely and in times of anxiety being a member of a temple and the scion of a priest-people. From day to day it is a matter of whom he dines with, exchanges calls with, plays cards with in a club of a Sunday and feels most at ease with; it is a matter of wives' intimacies, social habits, preferences and prejudices. To these the personality-image of the Jews as a priest-people with a mission is added; its work is to compensate the members of this social enclave for the continually reawakened inferiority-feelings in the Christian environment. Seen objectively, being a reform Jew is being first of all a member of a social group among the Jews; only tangentially does it consist in being a member of a religious sect. Income level and diction are usually more definitive of religious affiliation than theology or even dietary habits.

In sum: the Jews of America fall, with respect to Judaism, into three broad divisions none of which shows any seeds of a vital future Judaism. These divisions, of course, break up into smaller ones that overlap, cross, interpenetrate and pull away. Of course, the larger ones have their harmonies as well as their antagonisms. But the spring and drive of these harmonies come from common enemies and inert affirmations. Efforts to awaken living positive purposes that shall integrate the diversities of American Jewry into a stable creative force in American life and culture seem so far to be lacking. Not that the Jewish communities of the land have not made and are not making distinguished contributions to the national spirit; I have discussed this matter elsewhere * and shall say no more about it here. But it is to be noted that these contributions are themselves by-products of negations and inertia, automatic responses of the old Jewish order to the transforming pressure of the new land, the new life and the new institutions. The negations are the defenses against recrudescent anti-Semitism, such, for example, as are manifest in the initial intention and developed policy of the American Jewish Committee and the organization and activity of the American Jewish Congress and the Joint Distribution Committee during the war and after. The inert affirmations are those repeated by temple and synagogue without enduring effect on the young. Endeavors to establish common living purposes

* *Culture and Democracy in the United States.* Boni and Liveright.

for Jewry are concentrated largely in the "federation movement," and in the post-war transformation of the Jewish Welfare Board into a Jewish Center activity. The federation movement is seeking to integrate both the remedial and the educational establishments of the different strata of the Jewish communities into co-ordinated wholes. The Jewish Center movement is co-ordinating the free activity of the different Hebrew Associations. But how are the people rallying to the federation movement? And, in view of the astounding numbers of Jews in the Christian Associations, what may be said of the power of the Hebrew Associations and Jewish Centers to draw and to hold the Jews?

Concerning Judaism, the young listen and look and turn away.

V

Not the young Jew alone is averted from the religion of his fathers. The secularization of life by science and by industry has been more rapid among the Jews: the Jews have had farther to go than their Christian neighbors; their renaissance did not come until the 19th century and they have been undergoing in a hundred years a transformation which the Christian world took four hundred to accomplish. Christian youth are as little concerned about religion as their Jewish contemporaries, and the prospects are that they will be even less concerned.* They need religion less. Members of the dominant community and carriers of the prevailing culture, their feelings of inferiority, when they have them, are private and personal, not due to membership in a social group and status

* The current conflict between fundamentalism and modernism is a sign of how radical and thoroughgoing is the transformation of mind that science and industry are effecting. It is a 20th-century Protestant reformation.

in a cultural tradition. Their needs which religion serves are the everlasting ones that render religion permanent among the institutions of civilization; the needs that arise wherever youth discovers in its time that the world is not a place which was made for it but one in which it happened and grows and must die; one in which it can keep alive only by everlastingly risking its life against the unknown. Man's religions rest, in fact, upon the insecurities of man; they are his adjustment to the unknown.

Now to the general insecurities which inhere in and constitute life, Jews find added those which derive from the character of the Christian salvational system and which irradiate by emotional contagion into the social habits of the most modern of thinkers and the conceptions of the most contemporary of the so-called social sciences. Jews need religion more in their contacts with the modern world and it serves them less. In the perspectives of science and industry the concepts of "the chosen people" and "the mission of Israel" are no longer adequate to compensate for the feelings of inferiority imposed by the Jewish status in Christian history. In the perspectives of science and history the more tangible differentia of Judaistic doctrine and ritual, the tradition of the Torah and the rabbis are felt to be irrelevant, the costumes, not the clothes, of life. The deep-lying emotions from which religions spring tend to choose amid the perspectives of science and industry a common language. The identities rather than the diversities of what is essential in religion come to the attention. Sectarian boundaries cease to be important and are overflowed. Churches federate. Churches hold community services. Differences of religion cease to matter. Differences in habit of life go on. The result is the mind and heart of Jonah Gutman.

And that is a pity.

VI

Why it is a pity that young Jews of heart and mind should be averted from Judaism involves more than natural loyalty to something that one has been brought up in and is, even in rebellion and denial, so intimately one's own. There are not in Judaism saving powers which other religions lack, beauties which other religions fail in, or truths they do not possess. "Under the aspect of eternity," or as a rabbi might say, in the sight of God, each religion is the peer of every other in existence and in value. But to have these equivalences is a very different thing from having the same nature. The religions of men are in this like the men whose religions they are. All men are equal before God, who because he is just can have no favorites. But precisely because they are equal, they cannot be identical. Precisely because they are equal it is in their diversities, their specific characters, their uniquenesses, that they signify. Their parity of status liberates and assures their variety of nature. And so it is with religion, more than with any other of the institutions of man, particularly than with science, against which religion is set in sharp contrast. For science is one and religion is many; science is abstract and general and impersonal, religion is concrete and historical and dramatic. Religion has been one of the institutions of civilization in which specific emotion and the plastic imagination, under the impact of time and place and circumstances, generate those creations whereby the heart of man clears itself of its burden and transforms the alien world into something of a home. Science understands nature and uses her; religion reconciles human nature to fate and itself. Religion tends therefore to be of the nearness and intimacies of human life, plural, passionate and varied, enchanneling and conserving the concrete spontaneities of private feeling and public recollection. It embodies and transmits more fully than science the personality of a people, its precious uniqueness.

Religions do so, of course, only where they are themselves alive. . . .

Such being the nature of religions, they rest, for their survival and development, upon education. They rest upon education in a way that science does not. As I have said in another connection,* religion "depends for continuance upon verbal and visual instruction . . . it differs from the arts and sciences in the fact that its essential theme or subject-matter is in no way part of the necessary manipulable stuffs of the daily life. Food, clothing, shelter, defense against disease and against enemies do not require this instruction for their existence as they require animal, vegetable and mineral objects. Religion, on the other hand, if once forgotten, cannot be renewed as a science as physics or mathematics or chemistry can, by manipulating afresh the natural materials of which it is analysis and knowledge. Chemistry is always probable because chemicals are always actual. A theology, on the contrary, is only accidental and possible; it is an artifact; there is no stuff in the nature of things that necessarily implies it and whence it can be renewed. Religions, therefore, . . . have to be formally taught, even to the masses."

Without education religions cannot survive. Whether, through education, they survive as archaeological curiosities or living faiths depends on the success with which the transmitted tradition and the residual dynamic life interpenetrate and become organically one; on the com-

* *Education, the Machine and the Worker,* pp. 20–21. New Republic Publishing Co.

pleteness with which the ancient symbol utters the present feelings, purging the heart, and easing it.

Other things being equal, then, the future of Judaism depends upon the agencies which transmit it. And the ability of the agencies derives from the wisdom and spirituality of the agents, from the excellency with which they cause the Jewish religious past to function in the katharsis of those emotions of the problematic Jewish present that the other institutions of the common life cannot release nor clarify. The future of Judaism depends on the educational institutions of Judaism, and these, in their hierarchies and sectarian variety—from the *cheder* and Sunday school to the theological seminary and Yeshivah; from the Hebrew Associations and Jewish Centers to the temples and synagogues—depend, not upon their wealth and the elaboration of their machinery, but upon the specific contemporary relevancy of the tradition they pass on. They are the official keepers and conservators of Judaism. Are they keeping a living organism or conserving a mummy?

The answer to this question that the curricula of the institutions of Jewish higher learning provide is not hopeful. Their catalogs, their courses of instruction, do not reveal that there exists among their governors and teachers the slightest awareness of a present Jewry in a present world with present problems. The curricula, even of the most recent, present the aspect of an intellectual morgue, dedicated to the anatomy of the dead past of language and "law" and history. Nowhere is any realization indicated that the rabbi and the teacher must labor in a world of which industry, trade, science, the movies, the radio and the press are the dynamic substance, immediate and compelling. Nowhere is any realization indicated that the multiplicity and variety of contacts between Jew and non-Jew constantly increase and with them the aspects of "the Jewish problem." Nowhere is any realization indicated that Judaism is undergoing a progressive withdrawal from the organic totality of community life, that past and present, instead of interpenetrating and breeding the future together, are falling more and more apart, splitting the Jewish group-personality. The task before the rabbi and the teacher is to arrest this process, to reintegrate the duality into a single, harmonious whole. For the performance of this task, however, the discipline of the Jewish institutions of higher learning peculiarly unfits him. It accentuates rather than mitigates the split, and tends to drive Judaism farther from the modernities of the world.

VII

The last years of the late Col. Theodore Roosevelt's life were, as everybody will remember, years of stentorian crying-up of his own particular brand of Americanism— the *ne plus ultra* kind (later to be known as one hundred percentism), which insists upon the repression of variety no matter what its character.

Yet the Colonel died as all his life he had lived—a member of the *Dutch* Reformed Church.

This fact throws an interesting perspective on speculation concerning the future of Judaism in the United States. The point of departure is the precise meaning and weight, in fact and emotion, of the word "Dutch." What, in the matter of tone, of feeling, of behavior, does "Dutch" stand for in Roosevelt's biography? Mr. Bok, late of *The Ladies' Home Journal,* cites the Colonel as prideful of the Dutch aspect of his parentage, and as attributing excellences of temperament and conduct to it. But to the observer, at least, the Dutch color and flavoring of life, the

Dutch quality of cultivation and behavior had only the distinction of absence from the Colonel's stertorous existence. If it was knownly present at all, it was present in his inherited religious association; and whether it was there anything more than the label "Dutch" is a theoretical question. But for our purposes it is important to note that at least the label survived the manifold chances of cultural fortune which go under the eulogium "Americanization."

The fact is offered as aid and comfort for all the types of Judaist to whom Judaism is so precious that they would rather be distinguished from their neighbors by a sectarian label than by anything else at all. Let the whole living stuff of the complexus of practices, traditions, emotions, attitudes and sentiments which are enchanneled in the institutions of the various Jewish communities and make up their psyche, be worn to nothing; the temples and the synagogues will stand; the rabbis will preach; the choirs will sing in marble, even though vacant, halls— and there will still be the Chosen People, and their mission. Jewishness will be gone, but Judaism will survive. The priest-people will still be bearing testimony to the morals of Jehovah—through their rabbinical mouthpieces, in empty synagogues, of a Sunday—while they play pinochle at home or poker at the club.

The survival of such a Judaism, from which the body and richness and drive of a way of living have been refined away into the spirituality of a way of talking by a person hired for that purpose, may well continue indefinitely. Anything cut off from the moil and struggle of reality, from the clash of interests and causes, of loves and hungers and hates that make up the courses of the common life, can survive indefinitely. It can survive, but it cannot live.

Survival, then—the life-in-death of a mummy or a refrigerated fruit or a graveyard—is entirely open to Judaism, by whatever sectarian name it is called. As the ways of thinking and ways of behaving based on science and conditioned by industry enter into the texture of the daily life of Jews, Judaism and its institutions fall more and more into an innocuous desuetude. They are a charge against the community which the community pays out of deference to the past, out of a sort of ancestral piety, of the same memorial kind that evokes an annual *Kaddish*, and keeps a grave neat and trim and covered with flowers. They are a charge also for another cause, as pervasive but less noticeable, less easily recognized. It is fear of the future. The survival of Judaism is postulated upon the inertia of a respect for the past and the energy of a fear of the future. The former keeps it segregated and intact; that is, holy and therefore not to be drawn down into the mud and blood of the daily struggle. The latter requires it as a final insurance against the insecurities of fate and fortune of which everybody's biography is made up, and against the ultimate defeat of death.

Science and industry have provided tools wherewith we daily overcome fate and fortune, here a little, there a little. Disease and hunger and climate are not so competent against men as they used to be; even death, if the actuaries are to be trusted, has been somewhat put off. Science and industry, however, win merely life's battles. So far as any one person is concerned, they lose life's war. In everybody's history there are recurrent occasions when the best of his tools in his struggle with existence fail him. Basic hungers survive unsatisfied; impulses and energies and interests fundamental to our personalities are blocked or driven back or frustrated. Times come when the doctor can do no more and death cuts off even a Methusaleh; when the enemy is seen invincible; when the precious lost is at last irrecoverable, when there is no ease in the present, and no hope in the future that the visible world of science with its wisdom or industry with its engines can yield.

These times, times of actual or merely felt insecurity, or both, are the times when the engines of religion are drawn from their sacred retirement and put to work. The heart, in its restlessness or despair, returns from the modern secular instrumentalities which have failed it at last, to the ancient religious ones that had failed it before. If science cannot save me, religion must, hope, which is another name for the "will to live," tells the heart. If the doctor of medicine cannot heal, the healer of Christian Science shall, or perhaps Jehovah will respond to the psalmody of a pious *minyan* hired to mouth the songs of David, or to a special prayer. Anyhow, one can't lose anything; one will have done one's utmost, and salvation *may* come. . . . A miracle shall be, nevertheless, in this my so great need.

The technique that is thus invoked and set up is in principle the same for all sects—Christian Science, or Dutch Reformed, or Reformed Judaist, or Unitarian or Roman Catholic, or Sephard or Ashkenazi. It is the immemorial technique of religions—the technique of bringing to bear, by means of prayer or ritual or both, supernatural intervention in natural events. At its most sophisticated its defenders claim it is used simply to relieve the heart. It does relieve the heart, but I have never known a case where it was invoked merely for that purpose. All those which have come under my observation showed a hoping even against hope that a material change of fortune would be accomplished. At the very least, it served to pass on the responsibility for the desired change to powers beyond immediate personal direction. God's will had been invoked, and was to be done; thereafter, whatever the conclusion, there was an easing of the urge upon one's own will.

The instruments which one uses in order to influence God's will are, as every schoolboy knows, mostly very ancient. The rituals of the sacraments, the words and forms of prayer, the orative terms, are all sanctified and preserved against change. New sectaries may discard some parts and add others. But the new ones will be made to conform to the linguistic pattern or the dramatic pattern of the old. As nearly as possible, the quality and character of the instrument is passed on to the generations intact, unmodified by any use and uncontaminated by any circumstance. If this seems a paradox, in the light of the history of religions, with their reformations and revolutions and sectarian conflicts, let any honest-minded and candid candidate for the rabbinical degree undertake a circumstantial and comparative study of the ritual and prayer books of reform and orthodox Judaism. He will find that in so far as the reformed matter has content at all, it is a content whose pattern is merely an attenuation of the traditional one. That much of the language of the reform prayer book is a sort of English, makes it of course an addition to the ancient mode; and that the style of this English is cheap and occasionally vulgar and semi-literate is conceded. It would, however, hardly be fair to hold the tradition answerable for these virtues; it would be answerable only for the ideational content and the locutionary pattern. These, even in their vernacular vulgarization from Hebrew, become in their time automatically holy, and therefore inviolable to profane changes.

They, and the manners of conduct which compose a ritual, do of course change. But that change is another story. It falls outside of the intention of religion, and is a fate that even Roman Catholics are compelled to adjust themselves to. The gentlemen of the cloth make all the time, however, the pretense of inalterability. Orthodox clergy make this pretense for many things, reformers for fewer, but both make it. Both are conservators of traditional instruments of salvation. It is their stock in trade.

VIII

"Stock in trade" is not merely an "irreverent" label for the materials and formulae which make up the tools of Judaism. It is a term of accurate description. For Judaism is not a primary or fundamental interest of the totality, or even of a majority, of American Jewry. At its very best it is a reserve to be called on *in extremis;* at its worst it is a survival which persists because getting rid of it would be too much trouble. It belongs to the extreme and variable peripheries, not to the constant center of the life of American Jewish communities. Like more secular forms of insurance, its premiums are paid so that its implications may be ignored.

For one class of Jews, however, Judaism is of primary importance, near the core and center of life. This class is made up of all those who get a living by means of it, either directly or indirectly: the rabbis; the professors in theological schools; the undertakers; the *mohelim;* the Sunday school teachers; the *melamdim;* the *hazanim;* the *shochtim;* the owners and editors of "religious" papers; manufacturers of kosher sausages, soap or oil or sacramental wine; the matzoth bakers; the butchers; the *talith* and *mezuzah* and *tefillin* makers; the Torah writers; the *mikvah* keepers; the burial ground realtors—all the tertiary and quaternary *Keli-Kodesh* whose livelihoods derive directly or indirectly from the existence of the synagogue, the temple and their dependencies. They and their activities and products, their factories, embalming parlors, schools, colleges, graveyards and houses of prayer, compose a vested interest in the survival and perpetuation of Judaism. They are the ruling powers in the Judaistic economy. They must keep Judaism going in order to keep themselves going. To live, they must market their wares. They have, in spite of all sectarian and other differences, a common interest in making Judaism important and desirable to the Jews, their customers. Their interest in Judaism is active and constant, it is a professional interest; while the interest of the Jews in Judaism is passive and occasional, it is not even an amateur's interest.

To insure the survival of Judaism in the United States requires the transformation of this passive and occasional interest into an active and constant one. It requires getting the Jews to buy and use more of the items that actually compose Judaism over longer periods of time. It requires doing so in a competitive market, in which Judaism as a whole is not only engaged in a struggle for Jewish custom with Christian Science, Ethical Culture, Episcopalianism, Roman Catholicism and the modern point of view, but in which the different sects of Judaists are engaged in cutthroat competition with one another. In the latter respect, Judaists are even worse off than Protestants.

Indeed, among the Christian sectaries only the Roman Catholics have perfected anything like an organization that approaches toward maintaining a monopoly of its market for every variety of its goods—from the subtlest formulation of the mystery of the Trinity to the solidest miracle-working femur or protective amulet. Thought could advantageously be given to the highly centralized character of the priestly hierarchy and its autonomy, to the relation of its membership to church property, to its notion of "Catholic Truth" set over against other kinds, to its machinery of education, to its Index of proscribed books and its other devices for keeping its customers from solicitation by competitors, or for nullifying such solicitation.

However, it is so long since the Gaonate that hardly anything is possible on the Romanist model. For good or ill, Judaists are diversified into sects, and the prospect is very small of co-ordinating and unifying the activities of the Agudath Harabonim, the Free Synagogue, the United Synagogue of America, the Central Conference of American Rabbis, the Society for the Advancement of Judaism, the Jewish Science organizations, etc., etc. They are too bitter against each other to combine even against their non-Jewish competitors. And they would not know what to do if they did combine. The complexity of the interrelationship with the kosher food dealers, undertakers, burial-ground realtors, *et als*, would prove too confusing, and the curious circular movement of power and influence too elusive. This wants discussion, but I must for the present ignore these potent agencies in the survival of Judaism, and hope to return to an analysis of them on another occasion. For the present, I shall consider the factors that stick out above the surface—the schools of Judaism and the rabbinate. What can these do to make Judaism important to Jews?

IX

Have a look at an average rabbi of any of the three English-speaking sects—the reform, the "Schechter," and the Free Synagogue. His immediate background is, culturally, Yiddish; Judaistically, orthodox. The unremarked influences of his infancy and childhood, the agencies that have set him emotionally and intellectually, and have determined his attitudes of approach and withdrawal, expression and compensation, are of the inwardnesses of this background. They establish the pattern and the tonal values of his whole subsequent life, absorbing into their channels all the winnings of his education and later social experience. The education he has gotten has been conventionally sufficient. All three schools require from their candidates for rabbi some form of token for college discipline; they are, with variable meaning, graduate schools. At the very least the rabbi they turn out will have had the conventional courses in economics and literature and psychology and philosophy and sociology, and he will have been influenced by them in the usual way.

His choice of the rabbinate as a profession is not determined by any "vocation" not-to-be-denied. It has, as a rule, been made deliberately, after a survey and weighing of its alternatives—medicine, the law, engineering, etc. The effective motives for the choice are often not conscious. The fact that learning to be a rabbi usually costs nothing, that indeed it even very often brings one an income by way of subventions, scholarships, and incidental jobs, that in effect boys are bribed into the rabbinate as they are into Christian ministries, counts for a great deal. So does a certain privilege of status that accrues to the rabbinical student over against students in other callings. So does the relatively high income and the ease and security of life. The profession of rabbi calls for no great physical or intellectual exertion. It is exercised always under advantageous conditions. It calls for no risks of life, limb or income. It exempts its practitioner from the usual charges upon the maintenance of communal institutions —what rabbis contribute to the upkeep of hospitals, orphanages, schools, and other philanthropy would make an illuminating study in one phase of professional Judaism

—and entitles him to various emoluments and honoraria from circumcisions, confirmations, weddings, funerals and other solemnities and celebrations in the lives of his congregants. He gets a long vacation: from Shevuoth to Rosh Hashanah he leaves Jehovah unsolicited; his synagogue is usually closed and his flock unadmonished. His position in the larger community—not in relation to his Board of Directors—is one of honor and authority, for his profession renders him automatically the mouthpiece of Jewry to the Gentile world; he makes deliverances of the "the Jewish view" on anything, from Christmas to relativity, and none will dare challenge them, except another rabbi —or his Board of Directors.

His relation to this Board, and to the more powerful— that is, the wealthier—members of his congregation is a little more difficult than to the rest of the world. On the whole, he has to defer to them. He has to cultivate them, to make sure that his deliverances do not hurt their sensibilities or otherwise endanger his job. Or if he is free from the control of their views and needs, he is so because he has rendered himself important in the Gentile world, and has so figured in municipal, rotarian, theatrical, social servicical, political or other public affairs, that it is less distinguished to fire him than to keep him. The less he has minded his business as a rabbi, or, in the language of the cloth, a "spiritual leader," the surer he is to be secure in the job of one. And as the job is at worst not exigent, he has plenty of time.

The present conduct of the business of rabbi is familiar. The routinal duties are those set by the weekly services and the Sunday school. Their high point is the sermon. This may range from Ma to Mahi provided that, on the whole and in the long run, in one connection or another, Judaists are sufficiently praised for their adherence to the priceless Judaism which the preacher professes. A great reward of enlightenment and delight is in store for any student who will analyze merely the published sermons by American rabbis for any period of time and estimate the proportion of flattery to other matters.

The non-routine duties of the rabbi are those which come closer to the exercise of what I have shown to be the essential religious function. For the discharge of those, therefore, he collects additional fees—mostly for officiating at weddings and funerals, and similar occasions of moment in life. But I have heard of gifts and fees for assisting at the setting of gravestones, circumcisions, memorials for the dead, confirmations, etc., etc. These are, it will be seen, the standardized and conventional crises to which all religions attach their sacraments.

The massive residue of unstandardized personal crises that fall between these traditional high-points and are usually much more momentous and needy of religion, the rabbi is as a rule kept out of. His functions as a "spiritual leader" are by and large exhausted by the collection of routinal and non-routine activities. For him, as for all other ministers, "spiritual" means anything that calls for his intervention by means of one or another of these activities, anything that brings out his professional behavior: non-spiritual or "material" is whatever doesn't.

But it should be clear that there exists a great gap between the "spiritual" interests which the rabbi serves and the living needs for religion that his congregants feel. This is why, in their crises, they turn from Judaism elsewhere. Sometimes rabbis will deny this fact. They will repress it when they can; I have even heard of a superlatively respectable leader of English-speaking orthodoxy threatening to prevent consideration by a meeting of rabbis of a review of youthful defection from the synagogue and of its causes. And it cannot be denied that the defensive technique falsely attributed to the ostrich is an altogether human one. Its only insufficiency is that it fails to protect its users from their enemies. Something, too, can, of course, be said for a rabbinical policy for Judaism which looks no farther ahead than the security of one's own lifetime; "after me the deluge" is a maxim not without honor in other professions besides that of "spiritual leadership"; but if it is not effectively covered up, it is dangerous. The rabbinate has not effectively covered it up, and this is why, on the whole, the rabbinate's status in the minds of the Jewish masses and the rising generation of Jewry is not unambiguously honorable. The ambiguity is intensified whenever the average practice of the average rabbi is viewed in the light of the average preachment from his average pulpit.

X

The contrast between pretension and power, practice and preachment, claim and conduct, which signalizes the rabbi, no less than any other clergy, is not the fault of the rabbi as a person. Neither are the other stigmata by which the gentlemen of the cloth are differentiated from men in other vocations. The professional characteristics are acquired characteristics; the same men in other businesses would, most likely, appear as sincere, as upstanding and as courageous as their fellows. Their peculiarities of person are functions of the peculiarities of their calling. And the peculiarities of their calling are imposed upon them by the social conditions under which they earn their livings through practicing their profession, and by the content and form of their training. What the essential pattern of the social conditions is I have indicated in the previous section. I turn now to the professional training of the "spiritual leader."

Remember, this leadership for which he is being trained is to be exercised in the year of Christian redemption 1925, and the year since the Judaist creation of the world 5686 and as long thereafter as he holds his position. Think of the people whom he is to lead in the spirit; what jobs they work at; what tools they work with; where and how they work; what their play and relaxation consist of; what dangers they run; what hopes they cherish; what fears they undergo; what sort of instruments they satisfy their residual cravings with. Think of the modern world of science and machinery.

Now have a look at the sort of thing the candidate for rabbi is required to learn in preparation for the exercise of his function as "spiritual leader" of Jews living at such a time, in such a world.

I have before me the catalogs of the three English-using rabbinical training schools—in the order of their ortho-doxy: the Jewish Theological Seminary of America, the Hebrew Union College, the Jewish Institute of Religion. The first of these need not at present detain us. When the Seminary was merged with the Jewish Theological Seminary Association, in 1902, the task which it set itself was:

The preservation in America of the knowledge and practice of historical Judaism, as ordained in the Law of Moses and expounded by the Prophets and Sages of Israel in Biblical and Talmudical writings.

It proposed to train rabbis only in furtherance of this purpose, not for "spiritual leadership" in the modern world. The ostensible function of the rabbis it trains would be that of curators and conservators of archaeological possessions, of hereditary habits and formulae, against the attrition of the forces of modernity. That they have failed in this task is notorious. That anything other than failure was impossible is self-evident. "Historical" Judaism in the United States shows a content considerably differentiated from "historical" Judaism in Europe. Keeping the ordinations of the "Law of Moses" and the expositions of the "Prophets and Sages" of Israel going in a world of newspapers, automobiles and radios has developed for them meanings their originators would have been aghast at—not double meanings merely, multiple meanings. Seeming to say or to do one thing and intending something else has become the whole technique by which the *practice* at least of "historical Judaism" is preserved in America. The *knowledge* of it is, of course, another matter. Even if the Jewish Theological Seminary supports no more than one scholar, who with unflinching scientific conscience makes available to Jews a knowledge of the fulness of the Jewish past, it is justified.

For that matter, so are the other seminaries. But their primary intention is not the preservation of the Judaistic past, it is the advancement of the Judaistic present, chiefly by training rabbis, "spiritual leaders." Here is what the catalog says about the purpose of the Hebrew Union College:

It is in the most literal sense of the word the creation of Isaac M. Wise. It was founded by him because of his supreme conviction that Judaism in America could live and grow only as a real and positive American Judaism. This American Judaism would rest

upon the firm foundation of the eternal and unchangeable principles of historic Judaism; it would
root itself deep in the traditions, the literature, the
life, beliefs, practices and aspirations of Israel; it
would maintain its unbroken continuity with Israel's
past, and in Israel's history it would find the unerring
guiding principles of its future life and growth; it
would maintain and cherish its bond of union and
brotherhood with Judaism and Jewry the world over.
But it would also recognize its duty of existence and
self-expression, and claim the rights and fulfil the
obligations which necessity and history conferred
upon it, of adapting itself to the life which its children must live as loyal citizens of this American nation and participants in and eager contributors to
evolving American civilization. Only with this conscious program could Judaism live and grow in America.

All this Dr. Wise saw clearly. He saw that there
was nothing incompatible in Judaism and Americanism. He saw also that to evolve this unique and positive American Judaism would be a slow and difficult
task. Leaders were and would ever be needed, men
versed in all the lore of Israel, but equally taught in
and impelled by the traditions and aims of American
life; who burned with a like passion for Judaism and
Americanism. Jewish life and American life, Jewish
education and American education, Jewish ideals and
American ideals must be welded together into one
living, compelling reality by men who could teach and
lead and create with authority and consecration.
These men must be recruited from the ranks of American Jewry; they must be trained and inspired in our
own rabbinical seminary; that they might know and

live and promote the spirit and influence of American Judaism. For this purpose Dr. Wise called the Hebrew Union College into being.

The Jewish Institute of Religion, again, was organized:

For the purpose of establishing and maintaining an institution to train, in liberal spirit, men and women for the Jewish ministry, research and community service; to study scientifically Jewish literature, history and religious experience, and to make available to the general public a constructive knowledge of Judaism, its spiritual and social ideals, its history and outlook and its contribution to the world's progress; to advance Jewish scholarship; to establish and maintain a library and to educate and train rabbis and teachers.

Now look at the courses of study offered, on one hand, by the institution that is designed "to preserve the past" and, on the other, by those that aim to meet the present and advance the future.

Leading to the Degree of Rabbi the courses are offered as follows:

	Jewish Theological Seminary (hours)	Hebrew Union College (points)	Jewish Institute of Religion (points)
Bible	27	22	22
Talmud	29	14	22
Codes	2		
Mediaeval Hebrew	4		12
Hebrew	9	3	16
Liturgy	2		2
Midrash........	1	7	7

	Jewish Theological Seminary (hours)	Hebrew Union College (points)	Jewish Institute of Religion (points)
Mediaeval Jewish Philosophy ...	4	10	
Homiletics	2	3	
Post-Biblical History	6	8	8
Literature	4		
Theology	1	7	
Hazanut	4		
Problems of the Rabinate	1		
Mediaeval Biblical Commentaries.		6	
Ethics		1	
Jewish Social Studies		5	
Music		2	
Elocution ... (hours not specified)		4	
Aramaic			4
Arabic			8
Religion			12
Education			4
Social Service ...			8

The subjects are listed as they appear in the catalogs. Practically, it will be seen, they cover the same fields. The Jewish Institute of Religion includes Ethics and Theology under Religion; Problems of the Rabbinate, Jewish Social Studies and Social Service are names for relatively the same content. All three institutions give approximately the same weight to Post-Biblical history: the Jewish

Theological Seminary allowing two hours for the period from the beginning of the fourteenth century to modern times; the Hebrew Union College two from the beginning of the seventeenth century to the present; the Jewish Institute of Religion four from the fall of the Second Temple to the present.

The extraordinary fact is, therefore, that so far as curricular content is concerned the difference between the fundamentalist seminary, the reformist college and the liberal institute is negligible. There are slight differences in weighting the content: "social service" bulks larger than "problems of the rabbinate," and of course the theological lectures will point current sectarian issues. The rabbis of the three sects, then, are required to learn approximately the same matter. We must look to the attitude toward this matter to find the sectarian variation; to the methods applied in treating and presenting it, to the use or rejection of the assumptions and tools of modern scientific scholarship, to the readiness to accept or reject its implications, regardless of where they lead. But the reformist institution certainly has reservations against following where scientific scholarship leads; and whether the liberal one can go without them remains to be seen. "The eternal and unchangeable principles of historic Judiasm" are rendered taboo to scientific method by their mere designation, if one could only get agreement as to what they are. Perhaps Dr. Cyrus Adler would not take Genesis to mean what it says any more literally than Dr. Julian Morgenstern or Dr. Stephen S. Wise. But that the disagreement lets science in is another story.

What is at present of moment is the fact that in spite of all the brave language about leadership and living Judaism in American life, welded together by rabbis, the rabbinical training has no specifically American or generally Jewish

as against Judaistic content, whether in method or attitude. It is a thing apart, preoccupied with a very little
beyond the remote past, and needing translation to get
present significance. Such translation, if taken in the spirit
of science, is often transformation, and transformation
of the kind that science implies is more than the vested
interest of the clergy can go.

The Jewish Publication Society's version of the Old
Testament illustrates the situation completely. It is as
disingenuous as the English Bible made by Episcopalians
or the Roman Catholics. Done by a board of editors,
representative of all Jewish sects, who presumably had
all the tools and results of scientific method at their
fingers' ends, it nevertheless is carefully guarded from
any of them that might adversely affect the vested interests of the tradition, and thousands of Jewish homes are
sanctified with an English translation of the Bible by
Jewish scholars which falls far behind the conventional
American version in the candor, sincerity and courage of
the scholarship. In a word, this Englished Bible is kept a
repository of Judaistic survivals, just as the rabbis are
trained to be curators of such survivals in the daily life
and to enjoy the emoluments therefrom flowing.

Only, while it is in the nature of religions, and so of
Judaism, to conserve survivals, it is also in their nature to
render them presently available for the preservation and
enhancement of life. The latter function is indispensable
to the persistence of the former. Judaism shows in the
United States an increasing morbidity because this latter
function does not get exercised.

XI

I would be the last to deny the difficulty of preserving
antiques intact and at the same time keeping them potent

and operative in the stream of current life. It is a task of the nature of having your cake and eating it too; it has the same intellectual and moral implications as the Christian doctrine of transubstantiation. It presents those who assume the task with a dilemma between doing nothing and doing double meanings. The mass of the rabbis naturally take the easiest way, and do nothing. When Christian example is too prominent in the press to be any longer ignored, they may allow themselves to adopt imitative "social programs" or safe non-committal expressions of good-will to this or that. Occasionally they may be forced by the presence of still undisillusioned younger men to debate a Jewish issue. But any decision they make will have that precious *universal*—Rabbi Samuel Schulman's most cherished eulogium—character which commits them to nothing that may alter their comfortable *status quo* save in the direction of more comfort.

Some individuals there are, however, to whom the easiest way does not yield a stabilizing satisfaction. Their inward conflicts carry them away beyond the surrender that the young men make after a few years. They attempt revisions of Judaism on their own, multiplying the troubles of their colleagues and by no means certainly finding their personal balance. Such rabbis, for example, are Mordecai M. Kaplan, Joel Blau, and James W. Wise.

Rabbi Kaplan is professor of homiletics in the Jewish Theological Seminary of America. He is principal of the Teachers' Institute maintained by that Seminary. He is the "spiritual leader" of the Society for the Advancement of Judaism. His revision of Judaism is the most matured, the most articulately expressed and the most concretely embodied that American Jewry possesses. It consists in applying the method of interpretation worked out by an extremely modernistic Baptist theologian at the University of Chicago to the doctrines and practices of Judaism. With the result that you keep on repeating the antique formulae, praying the traditional prayers, performing the traditional rituals, and otherwise comporting yourself as a historical Judaist, but you have stopped meaning the historical things by them. What Dr. Kaplan has in mind when he says "God" and what Dr. Cyrus Adler has in mind when he says "God," could be reduced to identity only by a miracle of transubstantiation. And so on down the line of the contents of "historical Judaism." That Dr. Kaplan remains the professor of homiletics at the fundamentalist Seminary and appears to be the most originative and influential mind there, or, for that matter, in the whole Synagogue, should light up considerably the actual character of the business of preserving "the knowledge and practice of historical Judaism," while the tale of his endeavor to give his doctrine concrete embodiment in a religious society should indicate to what degree his revision has been successfully workable.

Nor does the content of the revisions by Rabbis Joel Blau and James W. Wise encourage me to think that they, either, have found the secret of getting the masses of Jews and the Jewish young to care any more about Judaism than is shown by taking a look and passing on.

The fact is, I think, that the revisionist programs are as inadequate as the institutional ones. They all are concerned with communicating knowledge, such as it is, about Judaism, with preserving it, using it, modifying it, and so on. But they assume that the modern Jews whose "spiritual" needs the professional keepers of Judaistic antiquities are to serve by means of them, require no study or understanding. They are to be known by the rabbinical mind immediately and intuitively in the same absolute way that Rabbi Joel Blau knows his God. It is of record that the assumption is not vindicated by its results. Rabbis, as a class, develop through no fault of their own neither into scholars nor ministers. They are compelled by circumstances to develop into public flatterers of the powers on which their livelihood depends. Flattery is the sum of their "spiritual leadership."

XII

If "historical Judaism" is to be preserved as a continuous current of life and not as a dead antiquity, it is necessary to train the rabbi for this purpose. It is necessary that the rabbinical schools shall pay much less attention to the Judaism of the past, and much more attention to the Jew of the present. It is necessary that scholarship, which is scientific knowledge of the past, shall be separated from ministry, which is wise service of the present. The business of the rabbi is to minister religiously to the modern Jews. To equip him only with ancient rules and practices is as self-defeating as to teach a medical student about herbs but not about the human body to which they are to be administered. How can a doctor so trained be anything but a quack or chiropractor?

The starting-point for the training of a Judaist minister is the Jewish present, not the Jewish past. The rabbinical seminary should be organized on the same principle as a first-class medical school. It should aim to instruct candidates for the rabbinate in the structure and functions of Jewish communities. It should aim to make them understand the nature and the development of the institutional organs of the communities, their reciprocal influences, their health and their diseases, the points of crisis or strain or transformation in their development at which his ministrations might be called for. It should aim to do the same things with respect to the individual Jews who compose the communities, and whose personal fates are implicated in their aggregate destiny. It should pay particular attention to the psychopathology of their daily lives in which their being Jews is a factor and which therefore calls for ministrations of Judaism. A training school for Judaist ministers, in a word, would familiarize its trainees with that total fulness of the life of the Jewish people which I am accustomed to call Hebraism, and of which Judaism is a part, and but a small part. It would familiarize its trainees with this not merely indirectly, through books and lectures, but directly, through intimate personal contact, observation and analysis in the field. It would not segregate students in dormitories or lodgings. It would require them to spend two years of a four years' course in the field, observing, analyzing, studying, serving, as a medical student does under guidance of his professors in a hospital. It would help them thus to discover where and how Judaism may enter into the totality of Jewish life, not as an influence of conflict and disintegration, set up against all that is Jewish but not Judaism, but as an instrument of co-ordination and healing, which every live religion must be.

And it would teach them Judaism. But the Judaism that it would teach them would not be the substance of scholarship in language, law and doctrine as these are currently transmitted in the theological seminaries. The practice of research into the historical data of Judaism is no concern of ministers of Judaism. It is the concern of Jewish scholars. It is a concern separate and distinct from the training of ministers of Judaism; it needs and deserves development on its own account, in its own institutions. The findings of scholarship should be made available to Jewish ministers but they should be made available with reference to their vocations, not to the vocation of the scholars.

That is, the point of departure for past knowledge must be the present life of Jewry. Knowing first what it is, its development should be retraced backward, step by step, from the near to the remote. In the matter of history or Hebrew, for example, it is much more important for the rabbi to know the last hundred years of the Jewish story than the first thousand, for causes lose in significance in proportion to their remoteness from effects. Thus the rabbi will be able to use the Judaism he has learned instead of being compelled, as he now is, by the necessities of his practice, to let it fall into desuetude. He will be able to bring it relevantly to bear as that device for the enhancement of security and the assuagement of fear which is the Jew's own and which is peculiarly suited therefore to the idiosyncrasy of any pathological condition or mood which arises within the structure and behavior patterns of Jewish groups.

I have now said enough. I realize that none of the three institutions whose courses I have surveyed is able, even if by some miracle its government were willing, to make such a change. Their investment in their *status quo* is too great; they have too many interests at stake.

In this respect they cannot do otherwise than corporations in other fields who are confronted with inventions that might lead to the scrapping of their present plants.

But it may be that some Jews of great wealth are interested enough in the persistence of Juadism as a living religion and not as an antique survival to risk some of their wealth on the experiment of bringing back Judaism to the Jew. For it is Judaism that must return to the Jew, not the Jew to Judaism. The whole history of Judaist institutions in America shows this. The transformations of orthodoxy, the mutations of reform, the appearance of new sects—these are not the activities of Jewish laymen. They are the endeavor of the churchmen, of the "spiritual leadership" to hold their customers, to catch up with the body of Jewry that keeps leaving them behind. Why they do not catch up and how they might, is what I have tried here to indicate.

More need not be added. The critical point in the survival of Judaism in the United States is the education of the professional Judaists, whose vocation is to bring Judaism livingly to bear at the moments in the lives of Jews where religious intervention is indicated. Once this is made relevant and adequate, the character of all the other institutions that transmit and preserve Judaism—the Sunday schools, Hebrew schools, etc.—would change correspondingly toward health and effectiveness. Until this is done, other efforts will simply spend themselves against institutional inertia.

I confess, sadly, that I have no great confidence that anybody who has the means and the power will have also the imagination and the courage to try to do it. Hope, nevertheless, springs eternal. . . .

1925

XVI

THE DYNAMICS OF THE JEWISH
CENTER *

The impression that comes to me through these sessions that I have attended with you is a mixed one. I get a feeling of considerable emotional tension. I get a feeling of the kind of confusion of mind that goes with emotional tension. I get a feeling of the theoretical blindness and practical groping, and I suspect that none of you will disagree with me if I say that the sessions themselves justify in no small degree Dr. Miller's characterization last evening † of the Jew as a person who is constantly analyzing his own motives and activities.

Analyzing can go on in two ways. It can go on with the speculative detachment of an observer who is taking the record and it can go on with all the anxiety patterns apparent that you seem to me to have shown throughout these sessions. Now, such anxiety patterns are in my judgment not peculiar at all to Jews who are engaged in the kind of work in which you are engaged. If it is any consolation to have company in your misery, then you may be assured that the Young Men's Christian Associations and the persons responsible for the destinies of those associations are in even a worse case. You may be assured that the rabbis and the clergymen are in a worse case than

* An Address at the Eleventh Annual Conference of the National Association of Jewish Community Center Secretaries.

† This reference is to the paper read at the session held Wednesday evening, June 5th, 1930.

the Young Men's Christian Associations. You may be assured that the problems of objective and of technique for obtaining objectives which exercise you are not peculiar to the Jewish situation in the United States at all, but are involved in the character of American institutional life as it exists today.

Let me stress that. And let me stress consequently that the general patterns of the solutions which are to be found to your problems are likely to be not so·very different from the general patterns of the solutions that will be found for the similar problems in the institutional life of the country as a whole. You can have a fair degree of confidence that those general patterns will be found. As Dr. Miller suggested last night, it may take at least 2,000 or 3,000 years for the energy of the upkeep of whatever we may mean by the term *Jewish* to exhaust itself; and anybody who bothers about the problem of a period of more than his own lifetime may be classed with those persons on the Island of Lupata who worried about when the sun would grow cold and were pickling sunbeams in cucumbers.

The eternal, even the secular, trend is significant only insofar as it can throw an illuminating perspective on actual activities and immediate problems. To secure such a perspective, what is most desirable is a certain historic sense of the forces in play, of the troublesome in the situation.

Now, I noticed that nobody who spoke in the sessions I attended seemed at all to raise the question of how and why the problem of the Jewish Center has developed as it has developed; yet the scientific procedure is automatically a historical procedure. I therefore decided this morning to venture into a field where I have no business. I do not know the history of the Jewish Center in such a way as to talk about it as a historian should, but I know enough about the general trends, both of the national life and of the life of Jewry in the United States, to know the pattern into which the forces fall that create the present situation.

Consider first the institutional background of the Jewish Center. You find it in two types of institutional activity; perhaps three types, but two certainly. The first of the two types is the Young Men's Hebrew Association. In its primary intention the Young Men's Hebrew Association was to be a Jewish parallel to the Young Men's Christian Association. The parallel is specific, and specific for every item of activity in the early history of the "Y's." In the beginning, the whole difference between the Young Men's Hebrew Association and the Young Men's Christian Association may have lain simply in what is implied by the term "Hebrew" and by the term "Christian." And in this connection most of what is implied is very close to nothing at all.

The other institutional activity—I think on the whole far more important than the first in its influence on the character and problems of the "Y"—is the social settlement, especially places of the type of the Educational Alliance on East Broadway in New York.

Now, the first intention of the social settlement and of the Educational Alliance was what in the course of time got to be known as "Americanization." The Alliance was a Jewish institution for making Jews over into Americans. In order to make Jews over into Americans you had to provide them with the necessary material and furniture by which an American is supposed to be defined. The programs of the settlement and of the Educational Alliance were therefore filled with all those various activities which seemed to have nothing whatsoever to do with

Jewish group life, which in fact are designed to divert Jews from Jewish group life into non-Jewish group life. For Americanization is a device for remodelling the minority which is different in the image of the ruling majority; and up to the war and beyond, the activity of Americanization, postulated on the constant stream of immigration into this country, is a swelling and mounting one which comes to a national climax in the admirable political record of that distinguished American, Warren G. Harding. Among the various forms it takes are what were known as the red raids and the other inventions and Americanization programs of such patriots as Mr. Palmer and Mr. Daugherty, the K.K.K. and the Daughters of the American Revolution. Those forms have since lapsed. There is no longer a department of Americanization in the national government. The craze is over, and the craze is over because to a certain degree the emotions that generated it have subsided and because the stream of immigration has dwindled down to almost nothing.

The next factor, the third factor, in the background of the Jewish Center, is the synagogue together with its activities. The synagogue and the activities of the synagogue are traditionally regarded as the foremost instruments in the upkeep of "Jewish group life on the highest possible plane." Yet from 1900 on it has been a growing experience of our "spiritual leaders," the rabbis, that somehow they were leaders with a progressively decreasing following. They found, as the same profession among the Christians found about Christianity, that in order to make Jews swallow Judaism it was necessary to sugar-coat the pill with what is called recreation. The first Jewish Center as such, so far as I know, was built by a synagogue; if I am not mistaken, by Rabbi Hirsch's synagogue in Chicago. And that Center, which was designed to serve as a reinforcement and accessory to the purely spiritual activities of the rabbinate among the rabbi's flock, somehow did not turn out in that way. The people who participated in the Center activities were not the people who participated in the activities of the Standard Club. They were not the people who participated in the natural Jewish group life of the Jews on the income level that could afford a pew in Rabbi Hirsch's synagogue. The persons who came to the Center were persons of a lower income level. They were persons from the West Side and from the fringes of the South Side and so on. The result was that after a while the Center took on the character and the pattern of something rather more like a social settlement and an Educational Alliance than of a Community Center for that particular parish whose spiritual leader was Rabbi Hirsch. I believe that on the whole this fact is true of practically all the Centers which are derivatives, direct derivatives, of synagogues.

The attempt to reinforce religious activity and interest with desirable secular activity and interest was not and cannot be said to this day to have been successful. It was experimental at the time the war broke out and the Jewish Welfare Board was constituted. When the war ended there came into play another factor of great importance in the development of the Jewish Center. That was the Jewish Welfare Board with unexpended money. Money is terribly important; it is no joke. Without money there is no Judaism; just as without a body there is no soul; without a violin there is no music. *Im ein kemach, ein Torah,* say the rabbis. Except in the case of God, you can't have a spirit in a vacuum. God, if the theologians report correctly, has neither body nor environment and is pure spirit, but everything else has some type of environment and is involved in some kind of physical, forceful relations with the environment. In modern society the symbol of such relations is money.

Well, the gentlemen of the Jewish Welfare Board were deeply concerned about the survival—I won't say of Jewish group life, to begin with, because that is a secular concept—but about the survival of Judaism in the United States. Deeply concerned. They felt that possibly, by a reintegration of these diverse, and on the whole, failing Judaistic activities, Jewish cohesion and that quality of the spirit (a quality which can be recognized but cannot be defined) that is called Jewish, might be preserved. They were ready to spend their money and energy on the work of preservation. Out of this readiness came the formulation of the Board's master objective, "the preservation of Jewish group life in America on the highest possible plane." Out of this interest and the combination of past circumstances and activities, the Jewish Center movement seems to me to have developed. If I am wrong please correct me.

II

I take it that the personnel of the Center movement were by no means trained to meet the special problems that that movement as such presented. Some of you came from social work or settlement work or Americanization work; others of you came from army welfare work, and so on. When a local organization was set going, you were called to your local jobs. And there you were. Set in the midst of a community to attain the grand objective of preserving Jewish group life in America on the highest possible plane without any preliminary analysis either of the character of the problem, of the resources available for meeting it, or of the situation in which the problem was to be met. Even under far more favorable conditions, how could a state of mind all confusion and groping fail to develop?

Let me remind you that the Center movement is only about ten years old and that perforce you are all still amateurs at the game. You are just learning your business and all learning involves a tremendous amount of fumblings and repetitions and what is called trial and error. These must come before you hit on the precise technique which accomplishes the end that you desire. Your situation does not therefore seem to me to be any cause for despair or any cause for doubting your objective. It is natural, and on the whole the persons in the analogous Christian movements with a much longer experience and much more expert at the game than you, are much worse off.

Well, you face a situation which sets you two problems, two tasks. The purpose of the Center movement is not one that your clientele needs to share with you. Fundamentally you are a missionary group. As the Christians say about their Christianity, your task is to "sell" Jewish group life to your clientele. Speak to any boy or girl or any grown-up that you might encounter in this Center about "Jewish group life." Would that person be able to define it for you any more than you seem to have been able to define it for yourselves? In point of fact there is no definition, for wherever Jews are together, wherever they are either cooperating together or quarreling together, there you have Jewish group life. Common activity of individuals working together is what makes a group; and individuals are usually prior.

Your task requires not only that you shall give your clientele what it wants, but that you shall teach them to want what you intend first and last to give them—"Jewish group life on the highest possible plane." The record of the activities of the different Centers seems to show that there is no such thing in the Centers. When you talk about "Jewish" activities you talk about a very limited percentage of courses or classes or lectures on Jewish subjects. Well, I know large bodies of Gentiles who also are preoccupied with Jewish subjects. . . . And then you have the very large proportion of activities which are glorified as athletics and recreation, and so on. These are the activities we have been hearing denounced as in no sense Jewish. But it seems to me that there is no cause for despair about those either, if you bear in mind how and why it is that these activities actually came into the Center.

The record indicates that, certainly in the large cities (and Jews are mostly urban people living in large cities), the Christian associations, the non-Jewish settlements, and so on, were drawing large numbers of young Jews. Even today the Jewish membership in the Christian "Y's" is very considerable. And one obvious procedure in the preservation of "Jewish group life" is to offer the young Jew, under Jewish auspices, the same thing that he is getting under Christian. The introduction of athletics and courses in culture and all these other things we have been hearing deplored is competitive. One way of conserving individual Jews to Jewish group life is by competitive imitation of the Christians. Ninety per cent. of the activity of the Center, as I see it today, has this character of competitive imitation. It is in direct competition for the custom of Jews with the non-Jewish institutions that have similar programs.

What happens when a Jew, for example, learns bookkeeping or stenography or accounting in a Jewish Center and not in a Y.M.C.A.? Objectively there is not anything to choose between the course given in the Christian association and the course given in the Jewish association. You might even have the same instructors. But, subjectively, a tremendous difference arises. The difference lies in the fact that the young Jew who goes to the Young Men's Christian Association is thereby committed to repressing as completely as may be his Jewish associations, his Jewish interests, his total attitude of Jew in Jewish social contacts. When he goes to the Community Center for the same activity he goes there consciously as a Jew because he is a Jew. That activity is at once emotionally stressed in a way quite different from the emotional stressing it receives in the Christian association.

Now, such emotional stressing is an extremely blind thing, yet it is the indispensable premise for the paradoxical transformation of the institutional aim that has come about since the 1900's. For whereas this type of institution began as an endeavor to de-Judaize the Jew, its endeavor today is to Judaize the Jew. The objective has become inverted. You have changed it from Americanization to Judaization.

The problem now is: Apart from the sense of belonging with Jews, what is the specific quality, the specific habit-form and thought-form in which this Judaization can take place so that bookkeeping can be Jewish bookkeeping, at least in the same sense in which relativity is Jewish? Yes, relativity is Jewish in a sense in which Bergsonism, for example, is not, and it is Jewish precisely because of the fact that Einstein belongs and knows he belongs and asserts the fact that he belongs to the Jewish group. Because Einstein as a person is involved constantly in making that difference which is the Jewish difference and Bergson is not. Yet relativity is far more abstract and universal in its content and far more unrelated to the Jewish tradition than Bergsonism, which is conceptually continuous with the Jewish philosophic outlook.

Here is a fact. Here is a fact for every individual who engages in any kind of impersonal activity: There is something in the posture of the mind, in the personal attitude, which colors the activity, which imparts to it a certain timbre. There is an emotional tone that distorts the material much or slightly, that throws it into a different perspective. Each people has such a timbre and such a tone. The Jews are no exception. For this reason you need make no excuse for aiming at large numbers of members. You should aim at large numbers of members. Every individual who is added to the collection, who consciously functions as a Jew in any activity whatever is thereby raw material for "Jewish group life on the highest possible plane."

III

Now, the problem as to what the actual content of Jewishness čan be, as it is projected into these apparently non-Jewish activities, is one that cannot be solved offhand. You don't know, and you are close to the job, and therefore necessarily without the perspective of the onlooker. I can't name it, although I have been watching the thing and am professionally concerned with perspectives. It is a problem which must be solved in the course of meeting it. We don't know effectively its premises. We don't know effectively its trends. All we know is that the Jewish Center is a battle instrument partly prepared in advance, partly developing out of the struggle of the Jewish group for survival in a social situation in which that survival is being constantly menaced.

One phase of this struggle consists in imitating the Christians. Another phase is the reproduction of the synagogal activity. Is my impression wrong that on the whole the rabbis feel competitive toward the Centers and urge that they should drop certain functions and leave it to the rabbis to go on failing to fulfil them? That there is on this point, as on many others, tension and strain within the group as well as tension and strain between the group and its social environment?

Competition by imitation is rather primitive, as well as traditionally Jewish. There are other modes of competitive activity. A group is defined by its competitive relationships quite as much as it is defined by its co-operative relationships, and the fact of struggle has an enormous influence on the sense of loyalty.

You read, for example, in the newspapers that the Hakoahs, who are no more Jewish fundamentally than Jack Dempsey, win a soccer game. You enjoy that record, don't you, simply because of the use of the Hebrew name "Hakoah" for this quite admirable business organization? The use of the competitive principle in athletics, in debates, in all the so-called recreational activities, is an important factor in the conservation of the group. Broadly speaking, anti-Semitism is an important factor, and if you wanted to be Machiavellian you could subsidize and cultivate anti-Semitism. But perhaps that will continue to take care of itself without any help from the Jews. You can postulate it as a fact to endure over a long period, certainly our lifetimes, and our lifetimes are all we need to consider, because they are all we can do anything in.

The residual problem remains: what, fundamentally, is "Jewish"? To this problem the answer is not to be found in the Center first off. It is to be found rather in the home, and in the relationship of the Center to the home. And the personality that dominates the home, even in modern times if you please, is the woman and not the man. The contemporary conservation of Jewish group life, so long as family organization is what it is, stays to a great degree the woman's function, for it involves postures of the mind and qualities of feeling that are developed basically in the first two or three years of an infant's life and are standardized and stereotyped in the next five or six. It seems to me, therefore, that there must be a fundamental shift in the incidence of your attack. Rabbi Robison said yesterday, if I remember correctly, that in Newark they were going to work with the adolescents. The adolescents are already more than a little too old. It is through the nursery and the kindergarten and the home that Jewish group life is preserved. The rest of the work that is done, the work that is done with persons who are over eighteen, who are post-adolescents, is a work of reenforcement and insurance. It serves rather to prevent drift than to develop a positive quality of character and conduct. The work of prevention, which, as I see it, is what you are doing now, rather than a work of construction, must go on. But more and more, infant education must become a Jewish charge on the Jewish community, and it can perfectly well become that because it comes in where there is no competition with the public school interest or public school activity. In later years competition expands rapidly and naturally. The Sunday school, the Cheder, and the Talmud Torah are secondary, not primary, interests to young Jewry and usually imposed, not chosen. But for the preschool child the educational work is primary because it is all.

IV

To organize this work and to face the problem, as it seems to me it should be faced, requires a considerable reorientation; first of all with respect to the intellectual content of Jewishness; secondly, respecting the emotional adjustment to habits, to mental attitudes, to things in the family life that invite invidious comparison with the external world.

The problem would be to find some core of unmistakable Jewishness which can become a nucleus able to assimilate the non-Jewish interests and activities. Assimilation, as you well know, can be two-sided. You can be assimilated and cease to be a Jew. You can assimilate and become universal and remain a Jew. The question is, which is to be the dominant and active process—the assimilation of the Jew by his social and intellectual environment or the assimilation of the social and intellectual environment by the Jew? By way of example, consider intermarriage. Some of you seemed to be disturbed about that. Yet that is not a problem except insofar as rabbis and a conventional fear have made it so. In the whole history of the Jewish people intermarriage has been constant. But about its effects nobody knows anything definite. Intermarriage may mean that the Jew who so marries subtracts himself from the Jewish group or it may mean the Jew who so marries adds another person to the Jewish group. When he adds another person to the Jewish group, the group is strengthened, at least numerically. And it is an ancient commonplace that persons who are members of a group by adoption and conscious intention are rather more intense in their loyalty than persons who are naturally of that group.

This, then, is the problem: to find a nucleus, a positive

Jewish nucleus of assimilation which can absorb personalities and principles, which can therefore keep the Jew
Jewish, and yet facilitate his contacts as an individual with
the non-Jewish world.

This problem can't be solved by discussion. It requires
careful study. It requires a research into the dynamics of
the Jewish group as it is today, a study of the incidence of
the non-Jewish factors, a study of the distortion that those
factors bring about in the present form of the Jewish community, and then a formulation of a technique by means of
which the undesirable distortions can be corrected and the
desirable ones can be emphasized and developed. There is
no foregone conclusion in this matter. It must be studied,
and after such a study has been completed—and it will
have to take a long time—the training of you lay rabbis can
properly begin.

Because you *are* lay rabbis. The Jewish Center arises in
the context of Jewish life because of the failure of the
Jewish Synagogue. It is a new organ designed to do the
same work. It has the characteristics which are evoked by
the new conditions that Jews are called upon to face and
that have rendered the synagogue no longer effective. Being new, of course, the Center is on trial. Of course it is
struggling for survival. But because it is new there is no
reason for despair. You need mostly a certain amount of
patience, a great deal of courage, and a sense of humor.

DISCUSSION

Bruno Lasker: The important thing for us to do is to
try and find out whether we are in agreement as to having
reached a new point of view, not a new objective but a
new view, a better understanding of the old objective,
and whether we can agree what that view implies in a

program either for the next year or over a number of years.

As I understand it, after giving us his excellent historical survey of the development of the ideals and practices of the Jewish Center movement, Mr. Kallen has shown that there has been a complete transformation of purpose in the past, perhaps five years ago; but what he did not clearly indicate, although he frequently seemed to imply it, is that we are again at a turning point, that while originally the Jewish social center was for de-Judaization and more lately was generally conceived to be an agency of Judaization, the problem now is how are we going to find out what Judaization means. How shall we go about to inject this Jewish ideal more and more into what otherwise might be entirely non-Jewish activities?

Mr. Kallen did not tell us or suggest where we might go for such a definition; but, it seems to me, he has suggested that the sources to which we used to go or to which some of us may have thought it was safe to go for authoritative knowledge of what is implied in Judaism, no longer exist for many of us, and that we have got to find out anew. And so perhaps having been a missionary center, as Mr. Kallen has pointed out, the social center must now become a center of study, a center for finding out. Finding out does not imply a missionary attitude, and the question is, to what extent you can combine that attitude with this new attitude which the disquiet of the discussion displayed yesterday, the new attitude of so many of us who want to rediscover the values of Judaism.

Therefore, it seems to me that possibly we might best start our discussion this morning by asking ourselves how we are going to go about that combination of objectives; on the one hand the endeavor to expose as many people as possible to Jewish influences simply by bringing them together with Jews—with activities definitely designed in a missionary spirit for concentrating Jewish influences on those contacts—and, on the other hand, the endeavor to find out for ourselves, for others and with others, exactly what this thing is which really will put Judaism on that "higher plane" that has been so much mentioned.

Dr. Cronbach: If I may ask a question, I will start the ball rolling. Is it to be expected that, in the course of the appreciably nearer future, the Center will make it possible for us to abandon the synagogue entirely?

Dr. Kallen: The question is, is it to be expected that the Center, if it is successful, may enable us to abandon the synagogue entirely? I think that it is likely to reduce the scope of the synagogue a great deal. But I don't think that any kind of activity can lead to a complete abandonment of what is usually called the religious interest. The reasons for that are not such as many rabbis would enjoy hearing. They have to do with a certain characteristic of our nature which makes us, when we are in very considerable difficulty, and all the usual resources, the secular resources, that might be brought to bear on solving that difficulty have failed, seek out supernatural or religious resources. You know, after people have been sick for a long time and some old woman comes along and says, "Why don't you go to see the rebbe?" they will say, "Well, I can't lose anything; I will go to the rebbe"—I beg your pardon, I should say to a Christian Science healer, shouldn't I? Or maybe the Jewish Science healer?

This kind of phenomenon is constantly recurrent. There is always a margin—it varies in extent and content—of insecurity and uncertainty in which the element of safety and certainty is introduced through the mediation either of the professional or the amateur religionist. Now, so long as the professional religionist is required, an institution will come with him, and so long the synagogue will survive. I think that that is likely to be about as long as the Jewish group survives.

Rabbi A. G. Robison: I should like to ask Dr. Kallen just what is this thing that we want to give our children under two years of age?

Dr. Kallen: I can't answer specifically because I have not yet myself succeeded in working out the kind of technique that I think desirable. . . .

Psychologically, the kitchen economy seems to be a far more important part of Jewish culture than the verbal economy. It is also the more important part of a child's life. Now, regardless of the fact that there is only one authentically Jewish dish, a dish which is associated with no other people, the matzoh, there is a kind of kitchen tradition which has been identified as Jewish just as another kind of kitchen tradition has been identified as English or another as American. That tradition is, of course, a function of the character of food supply and its accessories. Conditioning to the food supply, the upkeep of the technique of Kashruth, the sort of thing that Rabbi Kaplan is so heroically desiring and so interestingly failing in in New York City, seems to me an endeavor in the right direction. But there are no formulae at present. You see that is a matter of the home, of conditioning the child in infancy to certain tastes and interests. The thing has to be worked out. It sets problems in experimentation and in observation.

Rabbi H. Davidowitz: Rabbis are not hide-bound religionists in the evangelistic sense of the word in which their name seems to be taken at these gatherings. I will recall to your minds that in the olden days our rabbis were shoemakers and tailors and blacksmiths at the same time that they carried on their profession. I shall recall to your minds the good old Jewish rabbinic law that when one is engaged in study one is not supposed to interrupt his studies even for public prayer. The attitude that our people here take to the Jewish religion springs from a mistaken idea which the rabbis, some of us, have tried to rectify, but so far have failed.

They take their attitude of Judaism from the surrounding atmosphere, the attitude of Christians to their religion. In Judaism there was never any differentiation between what you call religion of the church or religion of the synagogue and the religion of the home or the folk ways. As a matter of fact, even today in America the rabbis continue the old tradition which was established at the time when the center of Jews was destroyed, when the rabbis got together in the house on the second floor of a member of their guild and decided that in order to preserve Jewish unity, Jewish life, it would be well to institute some laws regulating their food at home.

I will only call attention to the fact that although I am a rabbi, I on more than one occasion pointed out from my pulpit these very truths which were enumerated today, that Judaism is not to be found primarily in the synagogue, that Judaism does not start at Bar Mitzvah nor end there, that therefore it is most important that the mothers should learn what the teachings and traditions and history of Judaism are, and when they learn, without even interrupting their studies for synagogue, they will somehow find out how to transmit this, their knowledge, in terms of sentiment and emotion, to their little ones when they are with them; and I also stress this, that it is much more important for us to have Jewish kindergartens than it is to have Hillel foundations.

Milford Stern: As a lay board member, I am naturally

deeply interested in this discussion. Professor Kallen in his conclusion made a statement that executives of the Centers are lay rabbis and that the Centers have arisen because of the failure of the synagogues. In order to justify such conclusions I should like to ask Professor Kallen if he won't kindly tell us in a little more detail what factors make for the failure of the synagogue centers.

Dr. Kallen: I had said that the synagogue centers failed with respect to the membership of their own congregations. The reason for that is that the whole system of social life of the members of those synagogues which maintain Centers is concentrated on social clubs like the Standard Club in Chicago, or the Harmonie in New York, on golf clubs and card games and so on; you know the reform Jewish mode of living together as Jews. For the reformed, the synagogal activity is an activity which goes on at stated times and under certain conditions. Usually the membership is interested only when it is quite scared, that is, when it has to say Kaddish and on Yom Kippur. The interest stops at that point. Now the synagogue does not hold the interest or the allegiance of Jews. A continuous movement goes on from orthodoxy to conservatism, from conservatism to reform and thence to a certain quiescence, a kind of relaxation in reform which gets dissipated in one direction or another in christian science, in ethical culture and so on. The rest of the Jews are Jews or Judaists by inertia and not Jews by interest. I say "Judaists." I have been called to task in the public prints for having invented that word. May I remind you that today there is a very considerable body of Jews who do not believe in Judaism but are loyal Jews who believe in Jewishness, or as I prefer to say, in Hebraism. I do not believe in Judaism and I would be inclined to say that my friend, Mr. Lasker, does

not believe in Judaism. But I am very much interested in
Jewishness, and in Judaism as an item in the Hebraic tradition.

To be a Jew is one thing; to be a Judaist is another.
There are many Jews who are not Judaists and there
are some Judaists who are not Jews. The distinction is
forced on us. Now, Judaism is recessive for the same reason that among cultured classes Christianity is recessive.
The regression is a regression that is determined to a
considerable degree by altogether non-religious considera-
tions. Income is a factor. No less are the social aspirations
of wives in determining what Sunday school their children
will attend and whose children in Sunday school their
children will associate with. And last, of course, there are
the rhetorical and personal virtues of the rabbi. These
settle which temple or synagogue you belong to. The result: the rabbis find themselves, especially the rabbis who
speak for the kind of thing that Rabbi Davidowitz de-
fends and that I have a personal liking for, those rabbis
find themselves out of employment.

I have here, as it happens, the "Jewish Daily Bulletin"
for Friday, May 24th. This is a report from Belmar, N.
J.: "The apparent preference on the part of American
Jewry for Conservative and Reform religious affiliations
is menacing the earning capacity and livelihood of the
elder members of the Orthodox rabbinate, was the opinion stressed at the convention of the Union of Orthodox
Rabbis of the United States and Canada, which concluded
its sessions on Wednesday. The present state of the rabbinate on questions of Kashruth, on Sabbath observance
shared importance in the discussions. (*"Shared* importance" please note. And these should only "share" importance.) A number of rabbis unhesitatingly painted verbal
pictures of the deplorable conditions extant in communi-

ties throughout the country where rabbis, suffering loss of congregational adherents, are beginning to feel the effects, through decline of income and position. Rabbi Daichowitz, of New York, asserted that 'conditions in general of Orthodox rabbis of this country are worse than in Russia.' "

Well, the process here complained of is a continuous process. It is a process of secularization. The interest in the supernatural in this prosperous country, in the religious instrumentalities of survival, is necessarily a quiescent interest because there are few crises except death and serious disease which call for the intervention of the supernatural. Today, of course, many Jews, when they need the supernatural, will not turn to the rabbi, but to the Christian Science healer. Such is the social situation. As a general condition it is not peculiar to Jews, but it is a phase of the problem that we have come here to study.

Mr. Londow: I don't want to in any way trespass upon the privileges that I have already enjoyed in making various announcements and commenting upon different aspects of the activities of this conference, but there are certain trends of thought that have exhibited themselves here which suggest an attempt at restatement. It seems to me that what is involved in this whole question of duplication that concerns so many of our workers and the question of imitation, as Dr. Kallen put it to us, is the question as to what constitutes a good Jewish life. We heard last night something about the relationship of Jewish thought with monism and monotheism. Somehow or other, through all our thinking in all stages of our history, even in a conference of this kind, we seem to be groping for some sort of unified or centralized point of view, and this attempt to find some sort of formula that will satisfy the situation, or in the words of Dr. Soltes, a minimum acceptable program, seems to me to arise from this same philosophic tendency on the part of the Jewish mind. That being the case, it seems to me that we cannot leave here content with some perhaps logical and at the same time artificial attempt to differentiate between a Jew and a Judaist or a human being and a Jew, the distinction in the former case being made by Dr. Kallen and the distinction in the latter case by Dr. Cronbach. I think this attempt of trying to evaluate on the one side the secular activities of the Jewish Center and, on the other the so-called Jewish activities arises also from the endeavor to be logical. All these activities that we have in the Jewish Center, as we are thinking about them, are not necessarily logical processes, but as Mr. Glucksman has said again and again at these conferences, are biological facts, and these things that are going on arise from the fact that we express ourselves as human beings in these Centers. We are not at one moment Jews and at another moment human beings, but we are all the time people; we are Jews.

The interesting thing that is going on in Jewish life is not the attempt to get away from Judaism, but the tendency to include within Judaism newer and larger conceptions of what constitutes a good Jewish life; and these secular expressions on the part of our young people, it seems to me, are not an escape from Judaism but an attempt to enlarge the Jewish personality.

Let me take your time to try to explain how this thing strikes me. There was a time when a man living in a Jewish ghetto found himself completely happy by conforming to the practices of the Jewish code and his particular environment, and his various recreational and cultural and physical needs somehow or other, not knowing any better, were satisfied within that environment. Now, thanks to thought and the advance of science and these various other things that take place in the human spirit, we know more about what constitutes a good life. We know more about what it takes for a person to be healthy mentally and physically, what he really needs in order to be an adjusted individual in the complete sense of the word. We know today that if a person is to be healthy he must have an opportunity to make a living, and that is why we are interested in vocational education and adjustment. We know today that if a person is to be healthy he must have an opportunity to re-create himself after the exhaustion of his nervous and physical energy, and that is why we are interested in recreation as human beings. We know today that a person can find a great opportunity for studying his fellow beings through creative art, and that is why we are interested in dramatics. We know today that a person can express himself emotionally through music, and that is why we have choral societies and orchestras. These things are not anti-Jewish or exclusive of a Jewish spirit. They come to us because we have today a fuller appreciation of the comprehensiveness of human possibilities.

Judaism has always attempted to be coterminous with life or completely comprehensive of the values of human life, and that is why it seems to me that when we Jews are reaching out into the fields of dramatics and music and other activities we are not trying to express ourselves necessarily in non-Jewish ways, but as human beings in a constructive manner. From that standpoint I think our whole conception of Judaism is going through a transformation as a result of the enrichment of Jewish values and Jewish understanding through the enlargement of the field of Jewish activity within the Center.

Whenever you give Jews the opportunity of expressing themselves in any healthy way you have Jewish behaviorism. That is why I am not alarmed by the fact that our

Centers give courses in dramatics, in cooking or in brass-making. We are making Jews more healthy; we are making them more expressive; we are making them finer people. It seems to me there is no duplication here, and there is no competition.

What we want is that whenever a Jew expresses himself in any way he should somehow or other have within him that consciousness that he is living as a Jew, that he is aware of his kinship to the Jewish group, that he is aware of the possibilities of himself as an individual and the possibilities of his group of making some distinctive contribution to the welfare of the community at large; and whenever a Jewish Center does any creative piece of work in dramatics or in music or in physical education it makes a distinctive contribution to the culture of the community at large.

I think that what we need then is to understand a little better some of the conflicts that go on in the minds of the young people in America, so that we may help them to a clarification of their emotional and intellectual processes, to understand that when they are Jews they are at the same time, Dr. Cronbach, human beings.

Mr. Lasker: I think we should like to have Mr. Kallen reply to that part of the discussion which really was discussion, not questions, and tell us what, he feels, the whole discussion pointed up to.

Dr. Kallen: I like Mr. London's affirmative point of view, but it is a point of view which is dangerous if it involves ignoring the competitive background in which it arises and of which it seems to me to be a rationalization. It is comforting to say that what we are actually confronted with is an expansion of Jewish life, but if with this so-called expansion of Jewish life, Jewish quality becomes progressively diluted until it is unrecognizable, it is a dubious expansion; it is an expansion into nothing at all.

I think it is wise to bear in mind the competitive background of the social structure in which the Jewish community finds itself and to which the Jewish Center is a response. If you bear this in mind and then remember that it is necessary to discover—and that we don't know in the present situation what it is; we don't know and must needs discover it—that core of inherited Jewishness, that is, of socially transmitted Jewishness, which has the capacity for growth and for assimilating these external activities, so that when they are carried on they are by that fact made Jewish in the same sense in which your dinner, if you have a good digestion, is made into you. The fact is, of course, that when you have eaten and digested lamb, it is unrecognizable as lamb. It is you. Whatever you couldn't assimilate you have rejected and the machinery of rejection is as essential to life as the machinery of absorption. Indeed, one of the chief dangers, intellectual and otherwise, of all deliberations and assimilations is constipation.

Therefore, while I think that Mr. London is correct in principle, I think that that principle is likely, if you insist on it exclusively, to blind you to the events in the case out of which it arises. And such blindness would be suicidal. By all means, let Jewish life expand, but let the expansion sustain the continuity of Jewish being. Now, sustaining continuity is not preserving identity. You are not today what you were at the age of five. Your selfhood is a progressive system of variations and transformations from the beginning of your life to your end, and the sameness of you isn't a static identity. It is a process. And so long as that process goes on, eliminating what is unhealthy and dangerous to the organism, absorbing and assimilating the material of growth, you have a vital living individual. When there is any blocking of that process you have disease and trouble. Our present deliberations are testimony to the fact that there has been a blocking in the process of Jewish life rather than an expansion. We wouldn't have had these deliberations if there had been no blocking. And the problem is how to deal with it.

I can't repeat too often that there are no ready-made solutions of problems, just as there is never a ready-made attainment of any objective. You can't jump from the age of 5 to the age of 25; you can't skip the intervening years, you must live through them.

Those of you who read Yiddish, which is a part, if you please, of the Jewish tradition and culture, may remember a story by I. L. Peretz called "Bontsche Schweig." There is a profound moral for Jews in that story. Bontsche was a saint. He bore all his burdens, he endured all types of injustice and suffering, without complaining. So much so that by the time he was killed and so went to heaven, the angels in heaven and Jehovah himself couldn't prepare too great a welcome for him. If in that place Jimmy Walker had been alive and Mr. Whalen had been functioning, they no doubt would have been on the reception committee. Every possible perfection and expansion of life was available to Bontsche in heaven. He said, "You can't really mean me?" They said, "But we do. You can have anything you like." He said, "Anything?" "Sure." "Well, then, I will have a hot roll and butter every morning."

The tragedy of all the problems of the adjustment of means to ends, of separating ideals from instrumentalities, is summed up in that ultimate good which Bontsche asks for in heaven at the time when the whole universe is his to choose from. His choice is a tragedy because at no time during his earthly existence was he a healthy, growing, assimilative center. All he could do was to fix as his ideal something which he saw the other fellow have and which he had never had himself. What was therefore Paradise to him? A hot roll and butter. Now the Jewish community in the United States seems to me by way of getting stereotyped on hot rolls and butter, and the function ·of the Center or of somebody else who cares is to find out how the Center, which is one of American Jewry's newest instrumentalities of adjustment and expansion and conservation, can break up that stereotypy and really make Jewish life continuous and developing and expanding as Mr. Londow thinks it already is.

1930

XVII

RETROSPECT AND PROSPECT, 1932

Reading these papers over in order to get them ready for the press, it comes to me with a shock that the first of them dates back nearly twenty-five years. It was written at the instigation of Joseph Jacobs, to whom, together with Solomon Schechter, I owe more than to anybody else the definition and pattern of my interest and activity in the Jewish scene. In Jacobs, a peculiar quietude of spirit, a bystander's detachment combined with a deep and warm sympathy with this scene, moved me deeply; and Schechter's romantic militancy exercised a compelling contagion. Each managed in his own very personal way to fuse in his attitude toward Jewry and his vision of its destiny an idealism impressively free from illusion with a realism as impressively free from sordidness. On certain fundamentals I continue to differ as much from the one as from the other; we were friendly enemies, and both my mind and my method were kept sharpened by our happy combats. Perhaps those who hate me for what I observe and understand and describe as the Jewish scene should hate them also. I cannot separate their paternity of these perspectives from mine.

In the beginning, my rebellion against certain dominances in the scene (as must need be the case with all young people who respond earnestly to their vocation) was more intense than my integrations. I felt what I reacted against more deeply than what I pursued, and that in the Jewish world which I reacted against mostly, a quarter of a century ago, was the principle and program of reform Judaism as those came to me, not so much through its literature as through the personalities of its spokesmen and protagonists. The reaction led me to lay a much greater stress on the concepts of race and political autonomy than I do today. It reinforced the somewhat callow and hard realism which I opposed, not only to Judaism, but to religion as such. That, too, in the experiences and perspectives of nearly a quarter of a century has been mollified and dissolved. I am aware today of the mystic dimension and of its ineffables, and the years have brought me to a nearer insight and a sympathy with the indefeasible and unrealizable yearnings of the human heart and its pathetic and triumphant projections of its desires upon the irreconcilable world. I know now how intransigent is the making of illusions. . . .

For one thing, I have in these years come to a much nearer contact with rabbis. I realize that they are as different and varied individuals as other men and as little accountable for the deformations their profession imposes as lawyers or politicians. Especially, I have been impressed with the idealism and self-devotion of the generations of young men entering the study for the rabbinate. I have been saddened by the piteous distortions that the practice of their vocation effects upon them in a short time, and I have wondered what could be done not merely to preserve the qualities the young men start with from this ironic transformation, but to enhance and to fructify them.

Again, I am no longer the eager and perhaps intolerant Zionist I used to be. It is a decade since I have ceased to be a member of the Zionist organization. Indeed, events have forced upon my mind the reluctant conclusion that there is a conflict of interest between the building of a Jewish homeland and the upkeep of that organization, and I feel by no means so certain about the immediate prospects of this homeland as I did in the high and ardent days when we formulated "the Pittsburgh program" and envisioned with such assurance a new world of peace and freedom for all men that should come out of the war to end all wars. Fifteen years after the issue of the Balfour declaration, it is clear to me that the trend of social change and international politics in the Near East render extremely unlikely the proximate establishment on any significant scale of the Jewish homeland in Palestine. The mere ratio of births and deaths between Jews and Arabs points the moral. In the ten years, since the new Jewish settlement began, the natural increase of the Arabs has been twenty thousand, and the increase of the Jews both immigrant and native has been only nine thousand. . . . Nevertheless, I feel more clearly, more certainly than ever, how central the vision of the Jewish homeland is in the integrity of the personality-image of the Jews as a social group and how indispensable to its solidarity and survival is the effort to embody that vision in fact.

Even if the Zionist endeavor remain forever as unlikely of realization as it appears to be at the moment, it remains the ever-present and ever-unattained goal of the Jewish spirit so long as a single Jew is alive to carry on. For to abandon the vision of the homeland, is for Jewry to give up the ghost; it is to die because there is nothing to live for. A people, like an individual, has a personality which is focused in some particular ideal. Its whole life, like an individual's life, consists in the unremitting struggle to maintain this personality, to pursue the ideal. The end of every such struggle is necessarily death. Societies and nationalities are no more immortal than individual men and women. But neither the one nor the other dies by giving up the struggle voluntarily. The author of the Book of Job had a deep insight into both the psychology and the ethics here involved. "Behold, He will slay me," he makes his hero declare. "I have no hope. Nevertheless, I maintain my ways before Him. . . . Mine integrity hold I fast and will not let it go. My heart shall not reproach me so long as I live." I know not how many times I have cited these verses. They are the sum of wisdom to me, with respect to all things, and also with respect to the position of the Jews in relation to the Jewish homeland. The vision of the homeland is the center of Jewry's integrity. It must be held fast if Jewry is to survive as a sane people in what seems to be becoming an insane civilization. That, during such an effort, the fortune of events so often nullifies the logic of ideals is a fact to be recognized, but not surrendered to, whether in the relations between British, Jews and Arabs with respect to the Jewish homeland or in the definition of the Jewish position by Christian theology with respect to Jewish destiny everywhere else. Zion becomes more precious as Zionism becomes more futile. Discarnate in Palestine, it works salvation outside it, redeeming the Jew from the vanities of a moral materialism, the futilities of a life without root or direction. . . .

Thus, although my views have changed, they are not discontinuous. Rather, I trust, they have matured and mellowed, than been altered in insight and intention. . . .

Another thing that struck me as I came back to these works of my younger days was how much theology I had in fact been writing. I was not aware of this when responding to the several occasions that evoked the corresponding discussions. But there they are today, a redefinition, sketchy, perhaps, and as I see it now, more serious than perhaps need be, of Judaistic dogma in the light of modern trends in science and social life. So far as I know, in terms of any effect they may have had or any influence they exercised, they might as well have never been written. Yet the issues they deal with are as momentous, as urgent and as demanding of resolution as they ever were. Nay, more so. For forces whose impact was beginning to be felt in the dimmest way a quarter of a century ago are now in the field of consciousness of even the most complacent rabbi. Drifts and conflicts which a quarter of a century ago the "spiritual leaders" of Israel had either blinded themselves to, or were too unheeding to see, are now in the fulness of their flood. A new generation has come up which balks every effort to teach it the old formulae and postures, whether of reform or orthodoxy or conservatism or Zionism. It is moved by unexpected issues and to it the old ones come willy nilly empty of content and meaning. There is, I venture to believe, certainly a renewal of content and possibly a resurrection of meaning in the re-thinking of Judaism in terms of the modern point of view, in terms of the modern stress upon change and time as against eternity, upon individuality as against authority, upon plurality as against oneness, upon freedom as against regimentation. Anyhow, here is a beginning. Let the future do with it what it will. . . .

II

If the intellectual climate has changed by the recession of certain old interests and the emergence and diffusion of undeveloped ones, so has the social climate. Since the Great War, the configuration of the Jewish scene has acquired a new character. Rights for minorities that were written into the law of nations by the peace treaties designed to protect those corporate and cultural entities, have become sources of danger to Jewish life and culture because there exists no power effectively to enforce them. In such countries as Poland, Czecho-Slovakia, Rumania and Hungary, the Jewish position has grown steadily worse. The hatred of the Jews which Christian teaching ordains has been exacerbated and reinforced, on the one side by Jewish claims to equal rights which Jewry cannot make good, and on the other side by the general post-war economic disturbances of which the depression is at the moment the most acute phase. This disturbance tends to drain itself, in more civilized countries like Germany and Austria, in various forms of anti-Semitism, the usual effect of such disturbances so far as the Jews are concerned. The mediaeval practice of accusing them of causing whatever trouble the Christian community suffers from, is resumed at high pitch. Political parties are formed whose whole dynamic consists in reanimating the ancient Christian anger and attributing to the Jews the creation of all the ills they think they suffer from. Still again the Jew is assigned the position of the *Sair le'Azazel*, with whose elimination will be eliminated the ills of the world. Nazis and Cuzites may have positive programs as well as Jew-hatred, but the conditions are such that the desire to hurt somebody else is far more intense than the wish to better oneself, and the Jews are the traditionally convenient victims of this stronger desire. Even in Russia, where anti-Semitism is illegal and defined as counter-revolutionary, its manifestations have grown in scope and intensity since the early days of the Revolution. They appear in the ranks of the devout Communist party itself.

By contrast, Jewry in America looks both prosperous and secure. Yet signs of the old Christian malevolence have not been absent here either. People have not yet forgotten the henryford disseminations of the fantastic protocols of the elders of Zion, or the fulminations and marchings of the kukluxklan, or the agitation for the *numerus clausus* in more pretentious universities and colleges, or the economic discrimination against Jews or the various other indications of the vitality of the traditional Christian attitude in even this democratic, secular, and highly industrialized civilization. If the Jewish community has grown much in numbers, wealth and power, it has not grown much in security and organization. The one point on which a certain consensus of purpose and program has been reached is the upbuilding of the Jewish homeland. The establishment of the "Jewish agency" would be an event of the first importance, if the Zionist consent to it had not been so reluctant, and the non-Zionist participation so bored. But the attainment of even a formal unity is so unusual as to be a very significant thing.

One might add to that the growth and spread of "the federation movement" in many localities, if it were not for the fact that the communities in which the movement prevails seem no more integrated now than before it began. For the rest, the picture is one of drift and inconsequence, of reduplications and waste of effort, of a sort of blind running hither and thither to no purpose. Every group, every establishment, presses its own nostrum and its own primacy. We see the American Jewish Congress at war with the American Jewish Committee, and both pretending to act for a congeries of Jewish communities, most of whose members are not even aware that they exist. We see additions to the numbers and variety of Judaistic sects with the coming of "Jewish Science," which is some kind of Judaism distorted by contagion from Christian Science; and of the sect of the Free Synagogue captained by Stephen S. Wise and breeding its own special variety of rabbi in the Jewish Institute of Religion. We note the appearance of luxurious orthodox establishments with the full orthodox ritual and hardly a *minyan* at services. We note the contraction of orthodoxy among the poor; and the practical unchurching of the great majority of workingmen and workingwomen who are Judaists according to the U. S. census. We observe the endeavor to check the drift by means of "Jewish education" through educational associations engaged in "modernizing" the transmission of Hebrew and the rest to the new generations of Jews. We observe the Jewish Center movement with its endeavor to perform the task the synagogue is failing in, self-conscious, self-critical, uncertain of its goals and doubtful of its methods. And everlastingly there remain the charities which still do their great and disproportionate part in the upkeep of the Jews who cannot keep themselves up. We note the rise of an American Yiddish, the recession of the Yiddish press, the formation of societies to preserve Yiddish culture and many other such phenomena. There is great activity, but no action; great ferment, but no fertility. There is no singleness of purpose and no consensus concerning methods.

Under these conditions is it possible not to raise again the question, Can Judaism survive in the United States? . . .

It is not for me to attempt more of an answer to this question than I have already given. I wish only to go on record that I believe it can, and that I hope that it may. For as more and more human society moves toward uniformity of thought and work through the diffusion of science and of industry, human individuality, which is the most precious and indefeasible yet the most precarious value in the world, becomes surrounded by unprecedented dangers. Its very existence becomes a predicament, and it needs more varied and more numerous isles of security, reservoirs of life. Such isles, such reservoirs have in the past been nationalities, that is, group-personalities identified by common *mores* and common cultures; and I know of no alternative for the future. Among such nationalities, the Jewish has been outstanding, an extraordinarily labile and fruitful brotherhood, from whose families a disproportionate number of important individuals have, as Veblen observed, gone to bring their gifts to the larger ranges of civilization.

To maintain and enrich a function so signal is not called for. The conservation and prosperity of a mode of variation is enough.

Religion in America
Series II

An Arno Press Collection

Adler, Felix. **Creed and Deed:** A Series of Discourses. New York, 1877.

Alexander, Archibald. **Evidences of the Authenticity, Inspiration, and Canonical Authority of the Holy Scriptures.** Philadelphia, 1836.

Allen, Joseph Henry. **Our Liberal Movement in Theology:** Chiefly as Shown in Recollections of the History of Unitarianism in New England. 3rd edition. Boston, 1892.

American Temperance Society. **Permanent Temperance Documents of the American Temperance Society.** Boston, 1835.

American Tract Society. **The American Tract Society Documents,** 1824-1925. New York, 1972.

Bacon, Leonard. **The Genesis of the New England Churches.** New York, 1874.

Bartlett, S[amuel] C. **Historical Sketches of the Missions of the American Board.** New York, 1972.

Beecher, Lyman. **Lyman Beecher and the Reform of Society:** Four Sermons, 1804-1828. New York, 1972.

[Bishop, Isabella Lucy Bird.] **The Aspects of Religion in the United States of America.** London, 1859.

Bowden, James. **The History of the Society of Friends in America.** London, 1850, 1854. Two volumes in one.

Briggs, Charles Augustus. **Inaugural Address and Defense,** 1891-1893. New York, 1972.

Colwell, Stephen. **The Position of Christianity in the United States,** in Its Relations with Our Political Institutions, and Specially with Reference to Religious Instruction in the Public Schools. Philadelphia, 1854.

Dalcho, Frederick. **An Historical Account of the Protestant Episcopal Church, in South-Carolina,** from the First Settlement of the Province, to the War of the Revolution. Charleston, 1820.

Elliott, Walter. **The Life of Father Hecker.** New York, 1891.

Gibbons, James Cardinal. **A Retrospect of Fifty Years.** Baltimore, 1916. Two volumes in one.

Hammond, L[ily] H[ardy]. **Race and the South:** Two Studies, 1914-1922. New York, 1972.

Hayden, A[mos] S. **Early History of the Disciples in the Western Reserve, Ohio;** With Biographical Sketches of the Principal Agents in their Religious Movement. Cincinnati, 1875.

Hinke, William J., editor. **Life and Letters of the Rev. John Philip Boehm:** Founder of the Reformed Church in Pennsylvania, 1683-1749. Philadelphia, 1916.

Hopkins, Samuel. **A Treatise on the Millennium.** Boston, 1793.

Kallen, Horace M. **Judaism at Bay:** Essays Toward the Adjustment of Judaism to Modernity. New York, 1932.

Kreider, Harry Julius. **Lutheranism in Colonial New York.** New York, 1942.

Loughborough, J. N. **The Great Second Advent Movement:** Its Rise and Progress. Washington, 1905.

M'Clure, David and Elijah Parish. **Memoirs of the Rev. Eleazar Wheelock, D.D.** Newburyport, 1811.

McKinney, Richard I. **Religion in Higher Education Among Negroes.** New Haven, 1945.

Mayhew, Jonathan. **Observations on the Charter and Conduct of the Society for the Propagation of the Gospel in Foreign Parts;** Designed to Shew Their Non-conformity to Each Other. Boston, 1763.

Mott, John R. **The Evangelization of the World in this Generation.** New York, 1900.

Payne, Bishop Daniel A. **Sermons and Addresses,** 1853-1891. New York, 1972.

Phillips, C[harles] H. **The History of the Colored Methodist Episcopal Church in America:** Comprising Its Organization, Subsequent Development, and Present Status. Jackson, Tenn., 1898.

Reverend Elhanan Winchester: Biography and Letters. New York, 1972.

Riggs, Stephen R. **Tah-Koo Wah-Kan; Or, the Gospel Among the Dakotas.** Boston, 1869.

Rogers, Elder John. **The Biography of Eld. Barton Warren Stone, Written by Himself:** With Additions and Reflections. Cincinnati, 1847.

Booth-Tucker, Frederick. **The Salvation Army in America:** Selected Reports, 1899-1903. New York, 1972.

Satolli, Francis Archbishop. **Loyalty to Church and State.** Baltimore, 1895.

Schaff, Philip. **Church and State in the United States** or the American Idea of Religious Liberty and its Practical Effects with Official Documents. New York and London, 1888. (Reprinted from *Papers of the American Historical Association,* Vol. II, No. 4.)

Smith, Horace Wemyss. **Life and Correspondence of the Rev. William Smith, D.D.** Philadelphia, 1879, 1880. Two volumes in one.

Spalding, M[artin] J. **Sketches of the Early Catholic Missions of Kentucky;** From Their Commencement in 1787 to the Jubilee of 1826-7. Louisville, 1844.

Steiner, Bernard C., editor. **Rev. Thomas Bray:** His Life and Selected Works Relating to Maryland. Baltimore, 1901. (Reprinted from *Maryland Historical Society Fund Publication,* No. 37.)

To Win the West: Missionary Viewpoints, 1814-1815. New York, 1972.

Wayland, Francis and H. L. Wayland. **A Memoir of the Life and Labors of Francis Wayland, D.D., LL.D.** New York, 1867. Two volumes in one.

Willard, Frances E. **Woman and Temperance:** Or, the Work and Workers of the Woman's Christian Temperance Union. Hartford, 1883.